Only God
Can Deliver Like That

He Was Facing 12 Years
He Deserved Life
What He Got Was A Miracle

Thomas David Redlich

ISBN: 9781798485118

Imprint: Independently published

DEDICATION

To my four precious, priceless children whom God has so graciously blessed me with: Daddy loves you, Tommy, Danny, Brookie, and Rachael. Never forget that. It has been a tremendous blessing for me to be your father. My steadfast prayer and hope is that you will love the Lord Jesus with all your heart, soul, mind, and strength and that in the years to come, you will join your dad in proclaiming Jesus Christ as Savior, King, and Lord to a generation that is hopelessly lost without Him.

To my sons, Tommy and Daniel: I want to say that God clearly spoke to me concerning your future destiny in Christ. During a time of great personal distress when I had been anguishing in prayer for you, God told me in a dream, *"Your sons will not only be good men of God, but they will go on to be great men of God and soul-winners for the Lord."*

To my daughters, Brooke and Rachael, who are the delights of my heart: I want you to know that God's plan for you is to be His mouthpiece, so that you may minister love in the midst of hate and forgiveness in the midst of bitterness. You are to dance, sing, and proclaim the mercy and love of Christ to all who will hear. Remember, no matter what your problem or trial in life may be, God is greater and mightier than any obstacle or circumstance you will ever face.

ACKNOWLEDGMENTS

As Tom Redlich's defense attorney, I was a first-hand witness to the legal "miracle" that took place in the Milwaukee County judicial system when he faced the serious felony charges that were brought against him in 1985. The things that I saw take place from my front-row seat in these legal proceedings were truly unprecedented and cannot be defined as anything less than a sovereign act of God.

From the very first time that I met with Tom, I was impressed with his ever-growing and unwavering faith and trust in God. Despite his perilous legal position and the impossible odds that he was facing, Tom's strong faith that he would somehow be released from jail in time to be with his wife for the birth of their son was firm and undaunted throughout the criminal proceedings against him. Tom's living faith in God and the miraculous transformation that God had made in his life was acknowledged and given utmost consideration by the court system and the presiding judges involved in his cases. Tom's sincere faith and the complete transformation that had taken place in his life left a significant impression on the vice squad officers who arrested him and led to actions on their part that you will find to be truly incredible as you read this book.

Tom's loving faith and deep compassion for fellow inmates facing the wrath and punishment of the criminal justice system enabled him to be a blessing to many others during the time that he was in jail. To witness the flow of love and blessings being ministered to others from the depths of one who, at one time, was so hopelessly bound by crime and drugs was a wonder to behold.

To watch all of these events unfold from my unique vantage point as Tom's legal counsel was truly an amazing experience.

Sandy Stone Ruffalo
Attorney at Law

ACKNOWLEDGMENTS

In the early 1980's, the primary goal of the Milwaukee Vice Squad was to reduce the ever-increasing flow of cocaine into our city and to curtail the growing wave of crime and other destructive and disastrous activities that always accompany the increased availability and use of this highly addictive drug. We knew that Tom Redlich (alias Tom Wells) was a major source of cocaine coming into Milwaukee and that by arresting and prosecuting him (and his network of suppliers) we could significantly reduce the flow of illegal drugs into our city.

Arresting Tom and disabling his drug distribution network was a major priority for me and the Milwaukee Vice Squad Department for a number of years. We wanted him, and we wanted him bad! When we learned that he had been arrested in Montana and was being held there for extradition back to Milwaukee to face the charges that we had brought against him, we personally went there to bring him back to make sure that nothing went wrong. He had already eluded us once two years earlier when a major drug bust aimed at closing down his operation went awry. Now we had the opportunity to put him behind bars for twelve years and were determined not to let him get away from us again.

We took Tom into custody in Montana, handcuffed and shackled him and physically escorted him back to Milwaukee to face the felony charges against him. During our plane trip back to Milwaukee and during Tom's subsequent court appearances, certain dramatic and incredible events took place that you will never forget. You must read this book!

Detective Al Wilke
Milwaukee Vice Squad

ACKNOWLEDGMENTS

To Attorney Sandy Stone Ruffalo and Detective Al Wilke:

For your participation in the actual events described herein and your overall contribution to help make this book possible, thank you for allowing God to work the miracles through you that He performed. Your friendship, loyalty and willingness to go to bat for me – when I truly deserved to go to prison – will never be forgotten. Thank you for your willing involvement in this testimony and publication.

To Fred and Karen Genrich:

Only God knows what great treasures He has waiting for the two of you. And to Fred (who is truly one of the most gentle, kind, sensitive and generous Christians I have ever encountered) I want to say this: Thanks for going the second mile. Without your tireless work ethic, this project (and others still in the making) would not have come together as it has.

I can truly say that Jehovah Jireh is the Lord who looks ahead to provide. He graciously blessed me and allowed me to work with some of the finest Christians I have personally ever met. May the blessings of Almighty God be ever upon each of your lives, and may others continue to be impacted by your lives, talents, and testimonies according to the plan that He has for each of you.

Thomas D. Redlich

Contents

Forward

Tom Redlich is a dear and trusted friend whom I first met a number of years ago when the Lord led my wife and me to attend a service at "Ziklag World Ministries", his inner-city ministry in Milwaukee, Wisconsin. Tom Redlich is an extra-ordinary man with an extraordinary testimony, and he serves an awesome and extraordinary God – Jesus Christ, our Lord and Savior.

The Lord has called Tom to minister to those who live as he did before Jesus miraculously and powerfully transformed his life. He preaches to those who seek only the pleasures and answers that the world has to offer, ultimately finding themselves miserable, empty, and utterly forsaken by everyone and without any hope. His ministry is to the prison inmate, the drug dealer and addict, the alcoholic, the prostitute, the Christian who has "backslidden" and walked away from God, and to anyone else in need who will listen.

Tom Redlich is a living testimony of the unwavering love, mercy, grace, patience, and sustaining power of God available to the lost and perishing sinner, as well as to the rebellious and defiant "prodigal son" who has chosen to follow the way of the world instead of God's plan for his life. As a teenager, Tom Redlich was called by God to preach the saving Gospel of Jesus Christ. But just as with Jonah, who refused to heed the instructions that God gave him, Tom Redlich rejected the calling of God upon his life and went his own way to seek the respect and accolades of men and the wealth of this world. Also, as with Jonah, after much calamity and tribulation and after the occurrence of a very powerful and dramatic super-natural intervention by God in his life, Tom finally submitted to God's loving, perfect will and plan to use him as a soul winner, pastor and evangelist.

The story of Tom Redlich's early life, his serious and willful rebellion against God, and the dramatic supernatural events that caused him to return to the loving arms of his Savior is told in a separate publication entitled *Forgiven*. This current book, *Only God Can Deliver Like That*, relates the amazing events that occurred during the transitional period between Tom's return to the Lord and the beginning of his ministry to others. It covers the period when Tom had to "reap the harvest" of the vile seeds that he had sown during his period of rebellion, when he was driven by lust and greed to become a professional gambler and bookie, a major drug dealer, a drug addict, and armed robber, an associate of the syndicated crime underworld, and a "ladies man" who lived only to "party". It tells how Tom's firm faith, re-commitment and trust in Jesus took him through this very trying and difficult period, and how God, again, supernaturally intervened on his behalf to deliver him from impossible circumstances.

This book dramatically demonstrates how God can use the personal testimony of what Jesus has done in our own lives to impact the lives of others in a truly awesome way. God clearly shows us, through Tom's unique first-hand experience, that there is absolutely nothing that He is not able and willing to do on behalf of those who live and trust only in Him.

Tom Redlich's story is a living example of the truth of God's Word, which says, *"The Lord is on my side; I will not fear: what can man do unto me?"* (Psalm 118:6), and *"...If God be for us, who can be against us?"* (Romans 8:31).

Fred C. Genrich

1

Midnight Train
To Seattle

Hurriedly, I purchased my ticket and then boarded the Amtrak train, uniquely named the Empire Builder. My only possessions on this extraordinary trip were two heavy suitcases and an old army duffle bag. My one desire was to get out of town as fast as either plane or train could carry me. I tried my best to stay out of trouble's way and to keep myself as far removed from my darkened past as I could, but to no avail. I asked myself, *"Why didn't I listen to and fully obey the voice of Almighty God when He clearly commanded me, nearly two years earlier, to get as far away as I could from Milwaukee, Wisconsin"* (the scene of my criminal past)? God had told me, *"Get away from the drug pushers, junkies, pimps, prostitutes, players, gamblers, thieves, con artists and the proprietors of the dens of iniquity. Every one of them is a dead man, a walking sepulcher, and they have pulled you down to the very gates of hell. Leave Milwaukee, and get as far away as you can."*

With that riveting warning and clear direction from the Lord, I had left Milwaukee with my family, including my fiancee, Kristi, and our baby boy, Tommy. We moved to the tranquil, scenic setting of Amherst Junction, Wisconsin, to serve the Lord and begin our lives over again. I had intentionally distanced myself 150 miles from the Sodom and Gomorrah of my spurious past. Now only a handful of people knew of our whereabouts: yet somehow my past still caught up with me, and I soon realized that Amherst

Junction was not far enough away from Milwaukee as I had first believed it would be.

Just two days earlier, the sheriff's department sent a squad car over to our mobile home with a warrant for my arrest. The charges were completely unfounded. I was wanted for assault and battery regarding the beating of a major narcotics dealer in Milwaukee named Fred. I knew who they were talking about. Freddie and I had done business together in the past. The word was out on Freddie. He was marked as a thief and con artist. Many of his enemies had vowed to bury him. He had also betrayed me, and at one time I was out to smoke him. But now I was marching to the beat of a different drummer. Having pledged my allegiance to a forgiving Master, I knew that type of behavior (although very gratifying to my old "flesh" nature) would not be acceptable in Christ's loving eyes.

I couldn't figure it out. Why in the world would they arrest someone for roughing up a dope pusher – especially one of the most notorious around? I mean, this guy was a cut-throat maggot, the type that would sell T's and Blues (Slang term for a heroin substitute) to toddlers. The cops should have given out blue ribbons and an all-expense-paid trip to the Galapagos Islands to the man responsible for the pummeling of such a "law-abiding" citizen. Well, somehow my name got dropped in connection with his beating, and I wasn't going to wait around and get "popped" by the "fuzz."

God had a singular purpose and a mighty calling for my life. Deep in my heart I knew I was living far below the mark of excellence that was required of a good soldier of the Cross.

God was shaking me up so that I would finally obey His call and do His Holy bidding. He had told me, unequivocally, to leave Milwaukee and get as far away from the criminal element there as I could. Now it was high time for me to go and heed His voice. I knew immediately what I had to do. Although He didn't reveal to me exactly where to go, I remembered that He did say, *"Get as far away as you can."* I didn't need to look at a map. In times past I had looked at many maps, and I knew that the most distant point from Milwaukee could only mean Alaska.

I tenderly embraced Kristi as I told her and Tommy that Anchorage would be our future home. I planned to go there, get a job, get settled, and then send for them. I loved Kristi and Tommy with all of my being and dreaded any separation from them, but I knew in my heart this move was God's will for our lives.

Kristi tearfully drove me to the Greyhound bus depot in Stevens Point, Wisconsin, and bid me a sorrowful farewell. From there I traveled to Milwaukee and then took the Amtrak to Seattle. From Seattle I had planned to take the Alaska State Ferry to Anchorage. That train trip would last forty-four hours, virtually nonstop, and cover 2,123 miles of the most rugged, breathtaking terrain in America.

I had found a place to sit and relax on the crowded train, jam-packed with skiers who were hoping to get in one last ski trip before the winter snows melted. It was evening when the train left Milwaukee. I was looking forward to enjoying the scenery from the all-glass touring lounge car, but the sun had already set. In minutes the speeding train was engulfed in darkness.

It was a great relief to rest my head on the comfortable reclining seat. I reflected briefly on one other train trip I had taken to Las Vegas, but no other trip had nearly as much significance and purpose as this trip to Alaska. So much was at stake. I had fallen in love with a wonderful, trustworthy girl who loved me. She gave me everything I could ever ask for, and we were the proud parents of our first son, Tommy. Oh, what joy we shared together after his birth just seven months earlier! I longed to provide a happy, wholesome, God-filled life for my son and future bride.

The train ride had a soothing effect on my fatigued and frazzled nerves. Man, the pressure was really on now! I could feel the heat coming at me from all directions as if I were in the center of a hot, fiery furnace, and it hurt beyond description to leave my family behind.

Prior to this point in time, Kristi and I had never been separated from each other since we first fell in love four years earlier. To leave my home, my family, and my loved ones who depended upon me was one tough thing, but to be forced into this move because of a fraudulent warrant for my arrest was another.

All of this just didn't add up. It didn't make any sense. I felt like an angry, caged-up tiger, nervously pacing back and forth. Everything within me wanted to scream out, *"Let me out of this cage! Wake me up out of this terrifying nightmare!"* At the same time, God was decisively dealing with me. The firm voice of the Holy Spirit was convincing me that major areas in my life had to be dealt with. I needed to turn my back on the world and turn my face to Him. Sin has no place in a Christian's life. It must be repented of and left behind once and for all. Romans 6:14 says, *"For sin shall not have dominion over you, for you are not under the law, but under Grace."* In other words, God was telling me, in no uncertain terms, that I, Thomas Redlich (alias Thomas Wells), had to die. I needed to die to sin, die to the world, die to self, and pick up the Blood-stained Cross of Calvary.

Kristi and I had been soundly converted for well over a year, but somehow we slipped back into our old, selfish, carnal habits – habits that have no place for a child of the King. We needed desperately to find a church, but not just any church. We needed a sanctuary, a place of refuge, and a pastor that preached Jesus Christ and Him crucified. We needed a church that glorified and magnified the Holy Name of Jesus and believed in the all-atoning Blood of the Lamb of God that takes away the sin of the world. We needed to hear that God still saves to the "uttermost" and reaches out to the "gutter-most"; that… *The Lord's hand is not shortened that it cannot save; neither His ear heavy, that it cannot hear..."* (Isaiah 59:1); that Jesus still heals and delivers today; and that He is still "… *The Repairer of the breach, The Restorer of paths to dwell in"* (Isaiah 58:12). We needed to be reminded that only He can set the captive free and that the Holy Bible is God's Eternal Word. It was written by Him alone, and it is unchangeable. We needed to hear that even though this world and everything in it is going to pass away, God's Word will never pass away.

These were the teachings I learned and embraced as a child growing up in the Christian faith, teachings I heard my grandfather so powerfully and faithfully preach and heard my father so compassionately sing. I could never forget when Dad would sing my favorite hymn, "How Great Thou Art." I would watch intently as the congregation around me would weep because of the anointing upon my dad's gifted voice. Oh, how his voice and that song gave glory to God! This was what my priceless family and I needed more than anything.

After our move to Amherst Junction, we often watched our favorite Christian programs on television. God truly impacted our lives with the preaching of His Word. We began to earnestly hunger and thirst more and more for the Lord, but nothing could replace a church that we could call "home," with a loving, sensitive pastor, compassionate and forgiving people, and an altar where we could reach out and touch the hem of Christ's garment. Oh, how I missed the altars where our Holy God could be diligently sought and found and a person could walk away changed by the presence of the Holy Ghost.

Not a day had gone by, not even an hour, when my mind would not reflect back to the glorious day less than two years earlier when Father God had mercy upon my sin-sick soul and miraculously transformed my life. Make no mistake about it. At that time, I was horribly sick and thoroughly diseased. From the crown of my head to the soles of my feet, the grotesque, diabolical deformity of sin and spread its leprous lesions through me like a rampant, unstoppable cancer, leaving me hopelessly abandoned, raped, and mortally wounded.

On countless nights since that day when Jesus saved me and as I lay awake in bed with Kristi sound asleep beside me, my hands would grasp the Bible my father gave me when I was a young boy. I would hold God's Word tightly, pressed down hard upon my chest, and thank Him over and over again, worshiping Him for giving me another chance to live. I had fallen so dreadfully far away from God that my very soul was in the utmost danger of eternal wrath and damnation

What I've just described is only the beginning of the incredible story of what Jesus did for me when He powerfully intervened in my life and rescued me from my hopeless, sinful condition.

2

A Good Samaritan
Comes In The Night

As I was meditating on my sinful past that was redeemed by the precious Blood of Jesus, I heard the booming voice of one of the train employees shout out, "The dining coach will be serving dinner at 6:00, 7:00 and 8:00 pm! If you would like to have dinner tonight, you must eat at these designated times. The first call for supper will be in fifteen minutes."

I was famished, but more physically exhausted than I was hungry. I decided to rest for a while and catch dinner later. I dozed off for a couple of hours and woke up when the last call for supper was announced. I really didn't feel up to dinner that night, but I thought that a good steak would be just what the doctor ordered. I managed to pick myself up and walk the short distance to the diner car. I was somewhat relieved to see that it was relatively slow-paced and quiet. I didn't want to face a loud, standing-room-only crowd. I was promptly seated and began to browse through the menu selections.

As I pondered what I was going to order, I was interrupted by one of the waiters who seated a complete stranger at my table. I thought to myself, *Man, give me a break! I'm not in the mood for this. I don't want to eat with a stranger.* I knew from past experience that it was train policy to fill up all of the empty seats at each table first, so I reluctantly decided that I had to go along with it. I didn't want to rock the boat, so I kindly stretched out my hand and welcomed my uninvited guest.

His handshake was firm. His smile was inviting. It didn't take long to warm up to this affectionate intruder. He said softly, "My name is Tom Johnston. What's yours?"

"I'm Tommy Wells," I replied (which was the alias I was still using at that time). "It's a pleasure to meet you."

As I began to converse with this gentle giant of a man, I noticed that he was middle-aged, of medium height and he possessed a physique that rivaled the wrestlers on All-Star Wrestling. He must have weighed close to 240 pounds, and he had a big, round, rosy-cheeked face, a huge chest, and a portly midsection that reminded me of the ideal Santa Claus. Little did I know that this man would turn out to be the most cherished Christmas present I would ever receive.

We both ordered our food, and as I waited patiently for my T-bone steak, Tom spoke up, "What do you do for a living, Tom?"

Of all the questions in the world to ask, he had to ask me that. The one question that I was totally unable to answer. I honestly didn't know what to tell him.

The majority of my teen years were spent consumed in illegal gambling and bookmaking. Then at age nineteen I took a pivotal downward spiral by getting involved in major drug dealing and racketeering. I had close ties with people connected with the mob and dealt closely with other underworld organizations. At age twenty I got involved in a heinous crime that sent my life reeling to and fro like a rowboat caught in a violent typhoon: I committed an armed robbery with another man. I was arrested and faced a minimum of twenty-five years in prison with no possibility of parole. With only days separating me from my jury trial and an unavoidable prison sentence, God worked a miracle for me that prevented me from having to spend the best years of my life behind bars.

At this time, my life was being seriously threatened by known members of the underworld mob. With all hope slipping away and nowhere else to turn, the United States Government stepped in and placed me under the Witness Protection Program of the United

States Justice Department. My name and identity were changed, and I was secretly transported by armed bodyguards of the US. Marshal Service and relocated outside of my Milwaukee danger Zone.

A year later I was granted permission by the US. Justice Department to make my home in Las Vegas, Nevada. Now residing in the confines of the sin capital of the world. I became deeply entrenched in a lifestyle of gambling, gross sexual immorality, alcoholism, cocaine, and major narcotics dealing and use. I found myself totally bound and vexed by a myriad of vicious, vile sins.

I turned professional boxer for a short time under the skilled training and management of the former world middleweight boxing contender, Joey Giambra. Joey had the distinction of being called the "Uncrowned Middleweight Champion of the World." Through Joey's influential contacts, I became acquainted with power barons and other people I previously could have only dreamed of meeting. There were negotiations for a major motion picture about Joey's life, and I had the inside track to play the part of Joey during his illustrious boxing career.

I was soaring like an eagle and became involved in various business ventures: the casino business, bookmaking, major drug distribution, nightclubs, and restaurants. You name it, I tried it. In virtually every business I was involved with, the scenario always seemed to be the same. An initial period of great success and promise would ultimately be followed by resounding failure and disappointment. I now know that in each and every downfall I experienced, there was a common denominator that was the major contributing factor to the failure of my worldly business enterprises and endeavors. That common denominator was my Faithful and Loving God.

When I abandoned the Lord, I had become just like Gomer, the wife of Hosea, in the Bible. She walked away from her faithful husband and returned to the things of this world with passion by prostituting herself and trying desperately to find fulfillment and purpose with her adulterous lovers.

God compared her unfaithfulness to His own people, Israel, who also willfully walked away from Him and committed great spiritual whoredome by departing from His ways. In God's eyes this was treacherous and wrong. He said in Jeremiah 3:20, *"Surely as a wife treacherously departs from her husband, so have you dealt treacherously with me, O house of Israel."* And in Jeremiah 2:19 God said, *"Your own wickedness shall correct you, and your backslidings shall reprove you. Know therefore and see that it is an evil thing and bitter, that you have forsaken the Lord your God, and that my fear is not in you."*

But God moved in Gomer's life by putting a spiritual hedge of thorns and a protective wall around her so that she could not prosper in the wicked things she was pursuing. Only after she experienced enormous hardship and difficulty, which resulted from God's intervention in her life, were Gomer's eyes opened and her hard heart softened until she realized that everything she desired could be found in her God-fearing husband, Hosea.

God did the exact same thing to me when I became a backslider. I now understand why He did these things for Gomer, Israel, and me, out of sincere love, because we were not following His plan for our lives. He did it for our own good and welfare.

God loves me with a boundless love. He was willing to pursue me to the furthest extremity to restore our cherished relationship. God is a jealous God, and He was jealous over me because of the many things of this world that I had placed in a position of greater importance in my life than Him. Exodus 34:14 says, *"For the Lord, whose name is Jealous, is a jealous God."* Luke 19:10 says, *"For the Son of man is come to seek and to save that which was lost."* I was lost! But then Jesus came to find me. If I would have continued in my rebellious ways, my life would have been ultimately destroyed. I would have faced eternal separation from Him in the lake that burns with fire and brimstone. Romans 6:23 says, *"For the wages of sin is death, but the gift of God is eternal life through Jesus Christ our Lord."*

God put a spiritual hedge of thorns and a wall of protection around my life. Everything I purposed to do that was contrary to His plan, He would not allow to prosper. Businesses, associations, and pleasures outside of His will for me, He stopped. He allowed all of this to occur to bring hardship upon me so that I would repent and fall back upon Jesus, the Rock of my Salvation. Like the prodigal son, I came running back home to the outstretched arms of my loving Father.

In all of God's dealings with me, I had stopped up my ears and refused to listen to Him, and I continued in my wayward, rebellious path. With every business I started, the inevitable took place: a partner or friend would destroy the business through betrayal, deceit, or theft. These and other failures left me emotionally wounded, disillusioned, and financially bankrupt. But I never gave up: I never threw down the gloves and quit the fight. I always believed that the next time around I would make it to the top.

I had made innumerable trips throughout the country establishing drug connections in several major cities with some of the largest drug kingpins. At age twenty-five I began smuggling cocaine and marijuana out of Florida with one of the leading and most influential drug attorneys in Miami. With this major contact (and others I had secured throughout the years). I soon became a major drug supplier to the city of Milwaukee. During this time, my cocaine addiction became uncontrollable as I went from spending $100 a day to as much as $500 to $1000 a day to satisfy my drug needs.

Then a new and much more stimulating way of using cocaine had come fast upon the drug scene straight from the streets of the Big Apple. It was called freebasing, or crack smoking. The process involved purifying the cocaine powder into "rocks" using baking soda or ether and then smoking these "rocks" in a glass pipe, producing a euphoria of overpowering and unbelievable proportions.

I became a dealer-junkie, a pitiful slave and a stoned flunky, totally incarcerated by this form of drug use.

I spent a fortune supporting my ever-escalating drug fixation, which was enabled only by my lucrative drug enterprises and dealings with my affluent underworld clientele.

I spent years establishing connections with the most elite nightclub and private after-hours club entrepreneurs in Milwaukee. Some of the most talented entertainers in the city also purchased their product from me, and I even made a covenant with the head of the Black Mafia in Milwaukee that all drug purchases would come from me – and me alone. I consorted with other cartels and organizations with one goal in mind: to become the sole source of supply for their every cocaine, heroin, marijuana, and gambling need.

I finally reached the point where I felt the battle was lost. I felt absolutely powerless over this annihilating cocaine bondage that had me in its satanic claws. Alcohol had betrayed me, consuming me with delusions of madness. My life became a nightmare of uncontrollable drunkenness and licentious passions. Heroin, the venomous "white stallion," had become a constant riding companion that had turned on me, stomping and trampling over me with its hellish poison.

My insatiable appetite for riches, power, fame, greed, and lust had consumed me in its fiendish grip. These addictions of sin had also captured and tortured my friends' lives, minds, bodies and homes. Cocaine in this new crack form had taken the drug culture by a storm so fierce and volatile that everyone who crossed its path could ultimately be swept away to burn in the very pit of hell.

At the age of sixteen, I told Jesus, "There is no hope for me, God, no hope, for I have loved the things of this present world, and after them will I go." I was now twenty-eight, and in my wantonness for the wicked world, I thought I would find happiness and satisfaction. But I encountered nothing except grievous pain and lamentable turmoil. I lived a gruesome lifestyle that brought me face-to-face with death's door numerous times. I somehow strolled away from serious car accidents that should have left me paralyzed or a corpse. Likewise, I walked away unscratched from drug overdoses, drug ripoffs, and armed robberies where guns were held to my head. I was involved in countless fights. I was critically stabbed and almost bled to death. I was shot at, but never hit. I was involved in endless drug, gambling, and flagrant underworld racketeering schemes. I lived in a world where weapons and violence were a constant way of survival. It was a life filled with incessant fear of addiction, arrest, betrayal, failure, kidnapping, insanity, sickness, terror, and, worst of all, death.

I had drifted so far away from God that it appeared to all except One, my faithful friend, Jesus, that I would never come back to the Shepherd and Savior of my perishing soul.

I had finally reached a point that was unspeakably dreadful, a position so perilous and frightening that only God and I knew the incredible truth of what happened that fateful day when Jesus rescued my hell-bound life.

I now had so many questions and so few answers. I prayed earnestly for many months that God would send someone to guide and direct my path during this troubled time. Why did God allow me to live and not die? Why did He spare me from hell when I deserved to go there? What was His purpose for me in this lost and dying world? These questions, and many others, raced through my fatigued mind. There seemed to be so much confusion. I often prayed, *Oh, God, please send someone my way to help and guide me.*

As I contemplated my past, I remembered that Tom had just asked me what I did for a living. I decided to be honest with this man and said, "Tom, I'm at a loss for words. To tell the truth, I don't know what I do."

Tom scratched his head for a moment and just sat there silently with a puzzled look on his face. Then I spoke up and asked him the same question, "Tom, what do you do for a living?" I thought I would catch him off guard, but he quickly responded without even batting an eye.

He said, "Tom, I am a born-again Christian and a God-loving and God-fearing preacher man. I've been redeemed by the Blood of the Lamb, justified, sanctified, and glorified."

"I was miraculously saved out of the horrible pit of alcoholism and the miry clay of lust. I was enslaved to the things of this world and headed to a devil's hell. I was drinking myself to insanity and had lost all hope for life. I was utterly destitute and backslidden from God and covered from head to toe with sin and shame."

"I had become a vile man and was at the end of my rope when, in utter despair, I fell down on my knees and begged God to forgive me. Jesus reached down, and He saved me. He washed my sins in His Blood and heaved them into the 'sea of forgetfulness,' never to be remembered again."

"God then called this former backslider to preach the Gospel. And with every opportunity I get, I tell others of what Jesus has done for me." Tom exclaimed, *"'Let the Redeemed of the Lord say so, whom he hath redeemed from the hand of the enemy!'" (Psalm 107:2)*

As this blessed Good Samaritan poured out of his heart what God had done for him, the Lord revealed His fathomless love for me. He showed me how He had supernaturally orchestrated my unique meeting with this man. God answered my prayer and sent a man who could minister to my needs, a man who could help alleviate the roaring confusion that engulfed me.

At that time in my life, I was weary, confused, and carrying a heavy load. God said in Isaiah 50:4, *"I will speak a word in season to him that is weary."* The Lord divinely arranged our meeting on this train packed with hundreds of people, many who had never given their lives to Christ. He sovereignly united us on the diner coach at the third meal call, and then He put us at the same table so that He could be known to Tom and me and to all who hear this testimony as the prayer-answering God. He is El Shaddai, the All-Bountiful Supplier, the Breasted One, the Strong Nourisher, the Strong One, the Strength-Giver, the Life-Giver, the Fruitful One, the Satisfier, and the God Who Is More Than Enough.

Tom and I both shed tears of joy as he spoke about the great goodness and beauty of God. I cried out to this stranger, "Tom, I've been praying that God would send someone to me! I was also a backslider, and I desperately need to talk with you."

The moment I said those words, the yoke of confusion and discouragement that had been hanging over me was broken as the presence of the Holy Spirit swept over us. Then Tom placed his gentle, bear-like arms around me and embraced me, a fugitive on the run, saying, "Tom, I understand what you're going through, and the Lord has sent me here to help you." We wept arm-in-arm and heart-to-heart, praising and glorifying the King of Kings and the Lord of Lords.

God said In Isaiah 42:16, *"And I will bring the blind by a way that they knew not. I will lead them in paths that they have not known. I will make darkness light before them, and crooked things straight. These things will I do unto them, and not forsake them."* God has promised us, His children, in Hebrews 13:5, *"I will never leave thee, nor forsake thee."*

I knew I had found a friend for life, and I poured out my soul to Tom, telling him everything that was in my heart. He patiently listened and then poured out his heart to me. We became the best of friends over dinner that night and were virtually inseparable for the remainder of the trip. How I rejoiced that God answered my prayer and sent a man who could help resolve the questions that loomed over me!

Tom confided that he was a pastor in a small town near Hungry Horse, Montana, and his church and home were located just a few miles from the entrance of Glacier National Park. He was returning home from an important family meeting in his home state of Michigan, and his destination was Whitefish, Montana, where he would be picked up at the train station by his wife and two children.

Tom willingly ministered to me in love and compassion. We talked endlessly and prayed well into the wee hours of the morning until we finally fell asleep. The next day we continued to fellowship as we ate our meals together, prayed and, most importantly, discussed and read God's Holy Word. Tom's counsel, wisdom, and knowledge of the Bible brought a new-found strength in God for me, and his friendship would never be forgotten. I felt as though God had established a spiritual bond between the two of us, as He did with David and Jonathan in the Bible.

All that day we talked and laughed together, sharing our most intimate moments. I confided in him about why I was leaving the state of Wisconsin to go to Alaska with my family for a new start. I told him my story of how I had been born and raised in a loving Christian home and was committed to Christ at a tender young age. I was called to the ministry and then fell from grace when I backslid grievously and became a slave to sin. God dealt with me for years in love and mercy so that I would return to him. But I refused to listen.

I shared with him the heart-crushing story of Denny, my close friend who died a horrible, needless death because I wouldn't obey the voice of God. Jesus had unmistakably spoken to me, saying, *"Tom, tell Denny about Me. Tell him about My love. Tell him I died on the Cross of Calvary for him. Tell him I've come to set him free and that he should give his life to Me."* But because of my willful disobedience, tragedy struck just hours later in a drug house. Denny died instantly when he got caught in the crossfire of a gun battle and was accidentally shot in the forehead. God, in His limitless mercy, had warned me and given me one last chance to save my friend from death and an eternity in hell. I failed them both.

I poured out my heart to Tom, revealing all that took place during a two-week period of time when the Holy Spirit sovereignly dealt with me. God gave me a dream so terrifying that it rendered me speechless. Still, I wouldn't repent and turn from my sinful ways. Because of my willful rebellion, I left my Heavenly Father no choice. He visited me with His righteous pronouncement of unprecedented calamity, wrath, and judgment.

He opened the supernatural spirit realm to me. I saw sights and heard sounds so dreadful and frightening that no mortal could ever describe them. It was then, with all hope gone and my life hanging in the balance, with only seconds separating me from death and hell, that I heard the terrifying, resounding voice of Almighty God say, *"Tom, there is no hope for you. No hope. You have trampled upon the Blood of My Son and put Him to an open shame. This hour your life will be required of you."*

I had become like the maniac from Gadara, described in the fifth chapter of the Book of Mark, who lived in the tombs of the mountains. This man would cry out in anguish, screaming in bloody terror night and day. He would cut and scar himself with stones, trying to kill himself because of the awful torment of the six thousand demons who possessed him. Men would try to tame and bind him with chains, but he would break them asunder because of his supernatural, demonic strength.

I had also become the true proverb, *"The dog is turned to his own vomit again; and the sow that was washed to her wallowing in the mire"* (2 Peter 2:22). As I lay there prostrate, trembling in fear for my life with the Death Angel standing before me tolling the death bell, I begged God for mercy. I wept, begging and pleading with all of my strength and might that I would be given one more chance to live. Then Jesus my Savior, who is mighty to save, rushed to my side and had compassion upon me. He broke the chains of bondage and addiction in my life and forgave me of all my sin.

God the Father had visited me in righteous wrath and judgment, but Jesus intervened swiftly with mercy and grace to reconcile me to Him. I praise His Holy, Wonderful, Gloriously-Great Name. It was *"Amazing Grace! How sweet the sound that saved a wretch like me! I once was lost, but now am found, was blind, but now I see!"*

After sharing my testimony, Pastor Tom jumped up, exclaiming, "Tom, God has a great plan for your life. Any man that God rescues in such a mighty fashion, He is going to use in a powerful way. God's Word says that those who have been forgiven of much, love much. Never forget that, Tom."

Then Pastor Tom said something that I would never forget. "If things don't work out for you and your family in Alaska, I am giving you an open invitation to come to Montana and live with my family and me. If you ever have a problem, you can call me, and I will do my very best to help." Pastor Tom then wrote down his phone number and handed it to me, saying, "Tom, don't lose this number. Please call me collect if you ever have a problem or a need."

I was touched to be given such a warm invitation. There are few people in the world today that would stick out their necks for a stranger. Well, I sure didn't feel like a stranger to this Christ-loving and people-loving man anymore. We were no longer strangers, but we had become true friends.

The train was now just minutes away from Whitefish, Montana, where Tom would meet his waiting family. I would continue on my trip and probably never see him again. As the train began to slow down, I looked at Pastor Tom and told him, "I can't comprehend how God could have orchestrated our meeting, but I'm sure grateful that He did. I'm going to miss you, Pastor Tom."

We gave each other a bear hug and then said good-bye. As we parted, I began to chuckle and told Pastor Tom, "I don't know how this could be possible – it would have to be a miracle – but I feel that it's God's will for you to marry Kristi and me. Pastor Tom, I honestly feel that you will marry the two of us."

He answered with a grin, "Tom, it would be the greatest joy of my life to marry you and your lively bride."

The train stopped, and Pastor Tom got off into the cold chill of the night. A minute later I was surprised when he appeared back on the train and said excitedly, "Tommy, there's a ten-minute layover. Why don't you get off the train for a few minutes? I would like you to meet my wife and kids."

I jumped off the train into a raging winter blizzard. Pastor Tom enthusiastically introduced me to Sharon, his lovely wife, and his two daughters who were shivering in the blowing snow. I thanked God for loving me so much that he would give me a friend who spoke words of life, encouragement, and strength to me at a time when I was so heavily burdened and weary.

As I was about to board the train, Pastor Tom said, "Wait! We need to pray for you that God will grant you a blessed and safe trip." Pastor Tom's prayer touched the very portals of glory that night. When he finished, I leaped back on the train and waved good-bye to my God-sent Good Samaritan that came in the night.

I leaned back in my seat and reflected on God's goodness and then sunk back into a deep, restful sleep. I woke up the next day refreshed, feeling like a new man, and looking forward to the remainder of my trip. I couldn't help but acknowledge that, although this train was called the Empire Builder, that title so fittingly belonged to the King of Kings and the Lord of Lords who had begun anew to build His empire and kingdom in my life.

The train would be arriving in Seattle before noon, so for the rest of the morning, I just sat back and took in the celestial mountain ranges and snow-laden pines. Soon I would reach my first major destination, Seattle, Washington.

3

Crossroads In Seattle

Although the train trip was long and tiresome, meeting Pastor Tom had a life-changing effect upon me. I arrived in the major ocean port city of Seattle without any fanfare. I flagged down a cabby, instructing him to take me to an inexpensive hotel near the Alaska State Ferry dock.

I checked into a modest room and was anxious to see the town, but more importantly, I needed to book my reservation on the ferry, I asked the hotel manager where I could go to get a decent bite to eat. He told me, "Just two blocks down on the ocean front is the world-famous Pike Place Market. You'll find a variety of food and restaurants there that will blow you out of the water." Hey, I liked the sound of that. I love food, especially a great assortment of it, and I was definitely ready for this world-famous market.

After walking a short distance, I was amazed to see the vibrant enthusiasm of the business activity in the downtown Seattle area. People were hustling and bustling everywhere, and there was a sense of invigorating excitement in the air. As I walked along, I turned the corner, and there it was: the Pike Place Market. I moved into the crowded stream of people that was flowing in and out of this unique shopping mall and was spellbound when I saw the fish markets. Never before had I seen such a diversity of fresh, delectable seafood. There were salmon, shark, shrimp, king and Dungeness crab, oysters, lobster, and fish of every kind and dimension. All were superbly displayed to make one's mouth salivate all the way from Seattle to Hong Kong!

The produce markets were second-to-none. Because of my prior grocery and retail management experience, I knew a fair share about product presentation. These merchants at the Pike Place Market put me and the majority of my fellow entrepreneurs to shame.

This shopping experience was unrivaled by any that I had ever had. There were specialty-cut meat counters, boutiques, delicatessens, stores of all sorts and sizes, and restaurants where the food was sensational. I'm not a connoisseur, and I don't pretend to be, but my involvement in the food and beverage industry had left me with a fairly-seasoned, well-tempered palate. In other words, I could smell a great, tasty meal from a mile away.

I held a reputation among my peers in Milwaukee for making the best-tasting barbecued chicken and ribs that you have ever devoured. My seared, charcoal-grilled T-bone steak would have you singing, tap-dancing, and whistling all the way to Dixie. The slogan for my superb-tasting dishes was, "The barbecue is so good that it gets all over yo' hands and all in yo' hair."

For the next few hours, I drifted from one deli or food shop to another, sipping and sampling the savory delicacies and inhaling the atmosphere of this place. After Pike Place, I walked straight to the ferry dock and found that tickets were still available and affordable. I pulled out my wallet, ready to purchase a ticket, when the lady at the counter told me the next ferry would not be departing for ten days.

"Ten days!" I exclaimed. "you have got to be kidding. I can't wait ten days I need to get on that boat now."

A ten-day delay, with hotel and food costs, would leave me flat broke. As I went back to my room, disappointed and needing to figure out a new game plan, something more than my lack of finances began to bother me. I remembered the comments that I had overheard two train employees make about Anchorage. They spoke of the exorbitant rent, food, and utility expenses and said that many men were out of work.

At first, I wasn't overly concerned because I had never had a problem getting a good job in the past. I had extensive experience in the grocery, bar, restaurant, and casino industries. But the casino and bar business was an occupation I would never get involved in again.

All the glowing, glittering signs and shining, shimmering lights of the casinos and honky-tonks are a decadent delusion devised by the devil. This poisonous panorama paralyzes his unsuspecting prey and lures them to these gateways of demonic deception. He traps his willing victim through the greed of gambling and money, the lust of the flesh and the eyes, and the overindulgence of alcohol and drugs. Once he has someone in his snare, he viciously pounces upon his victim and mercilessly destroys all of the blessings, dreams, and loves of a man's heart.

John 10:10 says, *"The thief cometh not, but to steal, and to kill, and to destroy"* The devil is a treacherous, lying parasite who comes to take hostages and to massacre and slaughter God's children. If you place yourself under his guillotine and he takes your head off, you have no one to blame but yourself. God has warned man about the devil's tactics, and we are not ignorant of his devices. The Word of God says in 1 John 2:15-17, *"Love not the world, neither the things that are in the world. If any man love the world, the love of the Father is not in him. For all that is in the world, the lust of the flesh, and the lust of the eyes, and the pride of life, is not of the Father, but is of the world. And the world passes away, and the lust thereof, but he that does the will of God abideth for ever."* James 4:4 says, *"You adulterers and adulteresses, don't you know that the friendship of the world is enmity with God?"* Ephesians 5:11 says, *"And have no fellowship with the unfruitful works of darkness, but rather reprove them, for it is a shame even to speak of those things which are done of them in secret."*

I knew from painful experience the many pitfalls of this sordid way of life, and I didn't want to get involved in this lifestyle again.

4

A Cry For Help

As I walked back to my hotel room. I recalled a specific incident from my past that clearly portrayed how the addictive Las Vegas lifestyle can change and destroy people's lives and their relationships to those that they love.

I had worked at the Fremont Hotel and Casino for a couple of years as assistant manager of the race department and had made some good friends. One such friend was Danny, a respected blackjack dealer at Benny Binion's Horseshoe Hotel and Casino, located directly across the street from the Fremont in downtown Vegas.

After work, many employees of the race book would go to Binion's to party. It was *the* place to be. The Horseshoe was the hottest casino downtown, the place to eat, drink, carouse, and gamble. We all drank, and most of us gambled, but I often gambled until the sun came up. I was the life of the party. If there was a party anywhere, anyplace, anytime, you could bet your chips that Tom was there.

Binion's was always my first and last pit stop for the night. It was there that I met Danny. He was a kind, affectionate young man, full of life, Danny fell deeply in love with a dazzling "stone fox" named Rita. Danny helped Rita get blackjack training, and she quickly got a job. She first started working at the Lady Luck Casino and in no time, because of Danny's influence, was promoted to dealing at Binion's.

Everything looked promising for this young, attractive couple. Occasionally I would stop by their apartment, and we would have a few drinks together. Danny frequently bought his marijuana stash from me and we could always laugh and joke around together.

After a few months. I noticed that Rita loved to gamble. Danny and Rita often worked conflicting shifts, and many times I noticed that while Danny was working at Binion's, Rita was out playing blackjack. I always tried to give people I knew the benefit of the doubt. But I knew deep in my heart that Rita was in serious trouble, and I wanted to help.

During that time in my life, I was estranged from God. At various times, I noticed Christians in downtown Vegas passing out tracts and witnessing to the many people about the love of Christ. I would stand silently across the street and watch them, saying quietly within my heart, *Oh, God, bless those faithful Christians who so diligently share Your Holy Word. I remember in years gone by when I also passed out tracts and ministered the Good News about You. Even though I'm not serving You now, I know what these people are doing is right – and I'm wrong, dead wrong. All I ask is that you spare my life until I come back home. Jesus, You're still the best friend that I ever had.*

I often held back tears because Jesus never stopped calling me, but I just wouldn't come. I was so blinded and deceived by Satan that I believed his lie that my life would be worthless unless I accomplished my selfish goals. I had to become a millionaire, no matter what the cost. But I always knew deep in my heart that Jesus was the answer for my life and the lives of others.

I knew Rita was borrowing money from Danny to cover her gambling losses. Rita made good bucks an Binion's, and every dealer in Vegas knows that if you work at Binion's you can earn a good living. If Rita had to borrow money from Danny, I knew her gambling habit was now out of control.

In Vegas, it's a rule. You don't loan money to friends. Once you begin to borrow, everyone knows you're on a losing streak and it's just a matter of time before you get in over your head and get buried. I could see it in Rita's eyes, an addiction and bondage to gambling. She couldn't resist this blinding temptation. The world would say, "Tough luck. That's the way it is," and "She'll learn her lesson. She'll have to learn the hard way." The world is so cold, calculating, and merciless. It will chew you up and spit you out so fast it will make your head spin as if you got hit by a sucker punch from Mike Tyson.

Danny and Rita were in trouble, and I cared about them. I didn't want to see their hearts broken and their relationship come to an end. One day I noticed Rita walking through Binion's, and I got her attention. "Hey, Rita, what's going on? Do you have a minute? I would like to talk with you."

"Tom, I really can't talk right now," she said. "You probably heard that I lost my job, but I'll get another one. No problem."

"Listen, Rita, I'm not trying to pry into your life, but I've noticed that you're gambling too much. I just don't want to see you get burned."

"Thanks, Tom, but I'm doing just fine. I'll see you around."

I knew that Rita was lying, but there was nothing I could do. No doubt she lost her job because of gambling. I also knew from experience that her situation would get worse before it got better. A few days later when I saw Rita at the Mint Hotel and Casino, she said, "Hi, Tom, I need a big favor from you." I knew exactly what she was going to ask. "Tom, I'm broke. Could you loan me some cash?"

"No, Rita, I can't do that," I responded. "You're just going to blow the money, and I don't want to lose you as my friend."

She was desperate. "Listen, Tom, I really need some cash. I promise I'll pay you back tomorrow after Danny gets paid."

"No, Rita, I can't loan you any cash. I've lost too much money and too many friends in the past, and I don't want it to happen again."

When she realized I wasn't going to change my mind, she finally said, "All right, Tom, I understand. Could you buy me a drink, then?"

"Sure, Rita. Why don't you have a seat, and we can talk. Bartender, get Rita a drink."

We were making small talk for a minute, and then Rita said something that shook me to the very core and was a major reason why I decided to leave Vegas.

"Tom, I really appreciate the drink, but I'm in trouble. I need some money, and I need it right now. I've always known that you liked me. You always have. But because of Danny, you wouldn't make a pass at me. I'll make you a deal. If you give me the money I need. I'll go to bed with you, and I promise I'll never tell Danny. It will be our secret."

When Rita said those words, something in my heart broke for her and for every person like her. This lovely girl was willing to jeopardize her future marriage to Danny, trash her reputation with me, throw away any principles and morals she learned while growing up. And grieve her loving God, all because of a wretched bondage to gambling. Suddenly, I hated Vegas. I hated the casinos. I hated the casino owners and everything they stood for. I hated everything involved with this type of lifestyle.

I looked at Rita with pain in my eyes and told her that I could never do that to her or Danny. I was loyal to my friends and couldn't betray either of them.

As a loving and caring friend, I told Rita firmly, "You should be ashamed of yourself for allowing gambling to so dominate you that you would offer your body to the highest bidder. Can't you see how far you've fallen? If you don't watch out, soon you'll be hooking on the streets like a desperate prostitute. Sleeping with anybody you can so you can get your gambling fix."

"Tom, I wouldn't do that," she said. "I won't sleep with just anybody. But I will sleep with you, if you give me what I want."

I was really upset and finally told her, "Rita, don't you realize what you're saying? Didn't you hear what I just told you? Don't you know what you're doing? Please, just get away. Get out of my face. I don't want to see you again."

She looked stunned. Rita left, and I never saw her again. I sat there alone, feeling devastated and humiliated. At that moment, I hated this rotten, filthy world and everything in it. I hated Satan for his lewd wickedness. I told the Lord, "I'm getting out of this city, and I'm getting out right now."

I had had enough. I was tired of lives being destroyed right before my eyes. I knew the answer for Rita and Danny and others who were helplessly bound by sin. The answer was Jesus and He alone. Only through His precious Blood could this bondage be destroyed and forgiven. But because I was so backslidden and ashamed of my sinful, powerless life, I could not tell Rita of Jesus' saving and delivering power.

Oh, God, please send her a real Christian witness. Send someone who is not ashamed of Your Gospel, someone who is on fire for You, I prayed.

I now knew that this perilous lifestyle was a dead end street, and I could never go back to it again. I had made a commitment to Christ to never again be involved in any occupation that wasn't totally honest and upright. I knew the Lord would soon bless me with a job. One that would glorify Him.

As I meditated on these things on the way back to my hotel room in Seattle, I encountered a great host of people standing around, shouting and cheering. I learned they were there for the 1984 NCAA "Final Four" college Basketball Championships being played at the Kingdome. I had followed every college championship since I was a boy. I loved basketball and was a deadly shooting guard and captain for my school teams.

I became deeply involved in sports gambling at age fifteen, and since that time I had personally bet on and booked more college basketball games than most men alive. It was thrilling to be there during the "Final Four." I was beginning to imagine all kinds of schemes to scalp a ticket into the Kingdome, but I realized that no matter who was playing, I didn't have the cash to go to a game. Besides, it was far more important for me to find out if what I had heard about the problems in Alaska was true.

The next morning I inquired and found that the reports were true. The men in Anchorage who worked in the oil and fishing industries were out of work and spending most of their time getting drunk in the bars every day. Work was hard to find and rent and expenses difficult to pay, but I had set my heart on Alaska. I knew that if it was God's will for me to be there, He would somehow make a way.

During my brief ten-day Seattle excursion, I fell in love with this gateway to Alaska and the Orient. The spectacular Puget Sound Bay, the ethereal Olympic Mountains, beautiful Lake Washington, the luxuriant pines, and the tantalizing smell of spring flowers blooming in the air made this city a joy to visit. I enjoyed the magical downtown area with the Pike Place Market, the World's Fair Center, the 607-foot-high Space Needle, the Monorail train, and the Puget Sound ferries that daily transport thousands of cars across the bay area. I longed to stay. But my time here was now over, and I needed to prepare for my voyage on the ferry that was leaving the next morning.

5

Warning In The Night

As I fell fast asleep that last night in Seattle, the only thought on my mind was to board the ferry to Anchorage the next morning. During the night, God gave me a dream warning me of impending danger. I saw myself lying upon a bed located in a grassy courtyard in the middle of a large apartment complex. As I lay there in this strange, unfamiliar setting, I was filled with fear. I felt lost, frightened, and terribly alone. I began to run in terror, trying desperately to find out from someone, anyone, where I was and how to get home. I tried to speak to the few people that were there, but they only avoided me. Others mocked and humiliated me, pointing their fingers at me and laughing in scorn. In horror, I tried to find a place of safety and refuge, but to no avail. Finally, I woke up out of this nightmare, trembling. I heard the voice of God speak to my heart, warning me, *"Grave danger awaits you if you go to Anchorage. Check out of the hotel immediately and go straight to the train station. Call Pastor Tom from there. He will help you and give you guidance in the days ahead. Instead of Alaska, I am sending you to Montana to live."*

I got up at once and nervously packed my bags. I took a cab straight to the train station and immediately purchased a one-way ticket to Whitefish, Montana. I then called Pastor Tom.

He answered, "Hello, Tom Johnston speaking."

"Hi Pastor Tom, this is Tommy Wells, the young man you met

on the train. Please forgive me for calling so early, but last night I was all prepared and ready to board the ferry to Anchorage today, and God gave me a dream early this morning warning me of danger. Pastor Tom, God spoke to my heart to call you. He said that you would help me. Is that invitation to come to Montana and live with you still open?"

Pastor Tom said, "Tommy, I'm so grateful that you called. This is an answer to our prayers. Oh, Praise the Lord! Praise His mighty Name! You have been on my heart ever since we parted at the train station. God has also told me that you were to come here, and our church has been praying for you constantly since you left. Of course, the invitation is still open. When can you get here?"

I told him, "I'll be boarding the Amtrak in fifteen minutes and will arrive in Whitefish in thirteen and one-half hours. Will you pick me up at the station?"

"Sure, I'll pick you up. Oh, thank the Lord that you called and that you're safe. Tommy, I will see you soon. Have a good trip, and God bless you, son."

6

God's Big Sky Country

I boarded the train again, but this time I knew that my destination was chosen by God. Now I was headed for Whitefish, Montana. Man, serving God is a trip. I was beginning to realize that when you live for God, you should expect the unexpected. When I was following the ways of the world, I thought I was a "mover" and a "shaker". I thought I had it all together. But now I knew who the *Real* "Mover" and "Shaker" was.

I was shocked that God would give me a dream warning me of danger, but I was even more amazed that He gave me a way of escape by providing me a place of refuge with my new friend, Pastor Tom. It was going to be great to see how God would unfold His unique plan for me. The trip went quickly, and I soon arrived in Whitefish.

As I got off the train, I saw Pastor Tom waiting for me. It was dark and snowy when the train arrived, and I was exhausted. Tom warmly greeted me and said, "Welcome to Montana, Tommy. It's great to see you. This is truly an answer to prayer! I hope you like it here. Sharon and I fell in love with it years ago, and I pray that you will too. My wife has dinner waiting, so let's get out of this cold and go home."

I couldn't wait to see my new home, but we had to drive forty winding miles through drifting snow to get to Pastor Tom's house. When we finally arrived, his wife Sharon and their girls greeted me with hugs. We sat down for dinner, and Tom told me everything that he had arranged for me since we talked on the phone.

"Tommy, I've spoken with the owner of the cottage next door, and she's agreed to let you stay there. It's not the greatest, and it needs some work, but it will do until you get on your feet. Tomorrow I'll show you around, and hopefully, we'll get you a job, so don't worry about a thing. God's in charge."

Dinner was fabulous, but it was getting late, so Pastor Tom showed me to the cottage. I crashed hard on the pillow thanking God for His protection over me. I was looking forward to waking up the next morning to see what Montana was like.

When I woke up in the morning, I couldn't believe my eyes. I was surrounded by magnificent, snow-capped mountains. We were located just a few short miles from the entrance to Glacier National Park, one of the most scenic areas in the world, and I could see the glacier peaks in the distant sky. My God, this was a glorious place! I knocked at Pastor Tom's door, and he graciously invited me in.

He said, "Breakfast is on the stove. I hope you brought your appetite. So, what do you think of Montana now that you have seen it?"

"Pastor Tom, I wouldn't have believed it unless it was with my own eyes," I said. "This place is like Heaven!"

"Tommy, you ain't seen nothing yet! We've got a very busy day ahead of us. After breakfast, we'll go for a drive and I'll show you the greatness of our God." First, we went to Glacier National Park, then Hungry Horse Dam, and on to Whitefish where I saw, firsthand, the most breathtaking country my eyes had ever seen.

After the impressive sight-seeing tour. It was time for more serious business. Tom took me to a friend's ranch where he shot a steer, and I watched as he butchered it. With Pastor Tom's help, I found gainful employment working in the post yards. I also made an agreement with the landlord to rent the cottage I was staying in. We agreed that for one month's free rent, I would completely clean, carpet, and paint the cottage in preparation for the arrival of my family.

Just a few days had gone by, and I felt as though I had truly found a home, a place to raise my family, a loving pastor, and a church where I could grow in the things of God. Every day Pastor Tom's family and I ate together, and the bond between us grew stronger. As my first Sunday in Montana approached, I realized that it would be the very first time I had set foot in a real church in many backslidden years.

Everyone in church was glad to meet the man for whom they were so earnestly praying. God spoke directly to me through Pastor Tom's sermon, and at the end of the service, I rushed to the altar of mercy to seek the face of my Lord. It had been fifteen long, grievous years since I last knelt at a church altar and called on the Name of Jesus.

The Holy Spirit swept over me with waves of love, compassion, and glory. The heavy burden that I had carried for so long was dismantled by the gentleness of God. After a long time, I quietly got up and put my arms around Pastor Tom, thanking him for helping me get back to Jesus. I realized then just how important each person is in the "Body of Christ." We all can make a difference in the lives of others if we truly love God and other people.

I was grateful to be back with the Lord, and I couldn't wait to have Kristi and Tommy there with me. I had kept in constant communication with Kristi since I left Milwaukee. She was excited about what God had done and was eagerly anticipating the opportunity to rejoin me in the coming weeks.

7

As For Me And My House, We Will Serve The Lord

I wasted no time getting to work. My first job was posting, which involves the cutting and processing of a unique species of tree found in Montana and used specifically to make posts and poles. It was very dangerous and the most strenuous work I had ever done. Although it paid only a fraction of what I used to make as a drug dealer, I was grateful for the opportunity to do work that was pleasing to the Lord. Just a few weeks later, with the help of Pastor Tom, I was offered a construction job to help build an addition to a gas station.

I was able to begin saving money to bring my family to Montana, and I looked forward to their arrival. I couldn't wait to get Kristi and Tommy in my arms and hold them again to let them know how much I missed them. Montana was now our home. I made a commitment to serve the Lord with all of my heart, soul, mind, and strength. If He would enable me to bring my family here, I would raise them in the fear and admonition of the Lord. Like Joshua, I would take a stand and say, *"As for me and my house, we will serve the Lord"* (Joshua 24:15)

God was bestowing His blessings upon me in many ways, and I enjoyed the time alone with Him. I would often listen to preaching tapes that Pastor Tom had given me. How my heart was stirred as I listened to great warriors of God preach His matchless

Word. Every day I became spiritually stronger, and I knew God's hand was upon my life. Both Pastor Tom and I remembered the statement I had made on the train as he was about to get off. I had told him it would take a miracle, but I believed that someday he would marry Kristi and me. Well, that miracle was about to take place. We were already making preparations for our wedding, and I was working hard to get the cottage in suitable condition to be our new home.

It was early May when Kristi and Tommy finally arrived in Whitefish. Pastor Tom loaned me his old Cadillac to pick them up the night they came in on the train. It had been six long weeks since I had last seen them and thirty days since my arrival in Montana, but tonight we would be reunited again.

Moments after their train pulled into the Whitefish station, I was thrilled to see Kristi and Tommy come down the steps of the train right there in front of me. Tommy recognized me immediately and reached out for me to hold him. I embraced Kristi, and we delighted in our long-awaited reunion.

I told them both, "Welcome home, my darlings. Daddy has missed you so much." as we drove back to our cottage, located in the nearby town of Corum, I told Kristi, "Just wait until you see the immense beauty of our new home. It's too bad it's so dark out tonight. Tomorrow you'll see how truly beautiful it is."

After we arrived at the cottage, I helped Kristi and Tommy get settled and then went next door, briefly, to tell Pastor Tom that I would introduce my family to him in the morning.

Kristi woke up early the next morning, and we immediately walked outside to take in the breathtaking view. She was shocked when we first stepped outside and said, "This is even more beautiful than you described! This is a perfect place to raise our family. I can't wait to see everything!"

That morning I proudly introduced Kristi and Tommy to Pastor Tom. I was very pleased that he and Sharon could finally meet them. God began to work quickly and powerfully in our lives. In just two short weeks, Kristi made a re-commitment to Christ. She was baptized in Eagle's Lake, one of the bitter cold mountain lakes in our valley. She was also set free from an addictive smoking habit. It was exciting and reassuring for me to see her find joy and fulfillment in the things of God.

On Saturday, May 18, 1984, in Martin City, Montana, Kristi and I walked down the aisle of Pastor Tom's church and gave our lives to each other in holy matrimony in the sight of man and Almighty God. Kristi was the most ravishing bride I had ever seen, and marrying her fulfilled a lifelong dream. I had always wanted to marry a beautiful girl who loved Jesus as I did and to raise children who would love God and bless His Holy Name. This was my dream. In spite of my rebellion, God never gave up on me. He saved me and gave me another chance to fulfill His plan for my life. He also gave me the desire of my heart through my marriage to Kristi. How truly wonderful He Is! My son Tommy was my best man, which was an added benefit to this blessed day.

But truly, the "Best Man" was Jesus, the One who gave Himself as a willing sacrifice for the world. He was the *"Just"* who gave Himself for the *"unjust,"* so that all men could marvel at the abounding grace and love of God, *"For Christ also has once suffered for sins, the just for the unjust, that He might bring us to God, being put to death in the flesh, but quickened by the Spirit"* (1 Peter 3:18)

8

Chief Fat Bottom's

I was now a happily married man who was blessed with a wonderful wife and son. In addition, I was gainfully employed and excited about the future prospects for our new family. After the construction job I had been working on was finished, Ron, the new owner of Fred's gas and diesel service station, asked me to stay on as his employee. Fred's was a large, family-owned business and was considered a landmark. It was located on Highway 2, the main highway in that area, and nearly all of the passing tourists stopped there. Fred, the original owner, had retired and sold this "gold mine" to Ron. I took the job and pumped gas into the countless vehicles that made their last stop there before entering or exiting Glacier National Park. Despite the fact that I was only making five dollars an hour, Kristi and I somehow managed to get by. Ron paid me cash and gave me as much overtime as I wanted. Although pumping gas wasn't the greatest way to make a living, I was grateful to be alive. I knew that I would soon be promoted if I continued to work joyfully and faithfully unto the Lord with all of my strength in the job He had provided for me.

Directly across the street from Fred's was a large souvenir store and western bar that attracted many of the tens of thousands of tourists that came to see the matchless beauty of Glacier National Park during the summer months. Adjacent to the bar was an old log cabin ice-cream stand that had been shut down for two years. It was now early June, and every time I serviced a car, I would glance across the street and admire that little stand. I couldn't understand why no one wanted to take over that business and get it going again. It looked small from the outside and appeared to be cost-efficient. It seemed to me that it would probably be a profitable, low-overhead operation.

I thought to myself, Kristi and I could make this business go. I had no intention of making my job at Fred's a career, so I discussed going into this business with Kristi. She liked the idea.

I called the owner of the building and met her at the vacant ice-cream stand. After going over all the details, I made her an offer she couldn't refuse, and Kristi and I became the new managers of this unique outdoor ice-cream parlor.

The rent was affordable, and I became the biggest promoter this "Big Sky Country" had ever seen. With my schemes, Kristi's great looks, and God as our partner, we were an unbeatable team. Pastor Tom and Sharon were very supportive and completely behind us in our new business venture.

One day while at Pastor Tom's house eating lunch, we discussed our new enterprise. Always full of questions, he asked me, "Tom do you have a name for your business yet?"

"No, not yet, but I'm good at names. We'll have one in no time." I started rattling names off the top of my head, a mile a minute. All of them were clever and funny. Then everyone joined in with ideas, and all of us laughed together at whatever we came up with.

"Wait! I've got it!" I said suddenly. I announced to everyone that I had the perfect name for this new, up-and-coming entrepreneurial ice-cream venture. I had everyone at the edge of their seats, anxious to hear the name I had come up with.

"Now, listen up! This is the name of our new enterprise, and nobody is going to change my mind." Everyone was looking at me dead serious when I blurted out, "Chief Fat Bottom's!"

Looking a little bewildered, they asked, "Tom, how in the world did you come up with a name like that?"

"It's simple. Let me explain," I answered. "Montana is noted for its magnificent Indian heritage, right? The Blackfoot Indians have lived here for centuries, and at the head of every Indian tribe, there is a chief. Pastor Tom is the chief of our tribe and of our church, right? Also, Pastor Tom has got a big, fat bottom – a big, fat butt. That's how I got the name 'Chief Fat Bottom's'" Everyone was hysterical with laughter, and we all agreed that "Chief Fat Bottom's" was the perfect name.

In no time, we had the business up and running. Pastor Tom helped me design and construct a huge, colorful sign for our storefront. We also made a fifty-five-gallon-drum charcoal grill which I used to grill my favorite foods for our customers. This was the plan: Kristi would make the ice-cream cones, shakes, and sundaes, and I would flip on the grill and handle all of the cooking.

With the innumerable tourists that drove by, we needed something special that would make them stop dead in their tracks. So I created the Original Montana Buffalo Burger. We put up numerous signs along the highway leading right up to our stand, advertising "Chief Fat Bottom's Original Montana Buffalo Burgers" Virtually overnight, our business became a great success.

Kristi or I often carried little Tommy on our back as we made our customers their ice-cream cones or prepared the best-tasting Buffalo Burgers in the West for them. God blessed us. In no time, Kristi and I were making a good income. I told Him, "Thanks again, Lord, for Your help and for being Jehovah Jireh, 'the Lord that looks ahead to provide' for us."

We ran Chief Fat Bottom's through the summer and early fall months, enjoying the beautiful weather and serving the many tourists that came our way. With the great variety of people that came to Chief Fat Bottom's, there was never a dull moment. On our menu were delicious homemade Wisconsin bratwurst sandwiches, which we called "Brats." On one memorable and funny occasion, two Canadian tourists asked me, "What in the world are "Brats'?" I responded jokingly, "Your rotten kids who don't know how to behave themselves," and they laughed. I really enjoyed running this business with Kristi. We made a good team.

One customer that became a regular was Bob, the owner of the Hungry Horse IGA grocery store. He was originally from New

York City and loved my homemade Italian sausage. I told him about my prior grocery experience, and he asked me if I would like to work for him after the summer months. I told him I would consider his offer. Over the months that followed, we became good friends.

When the summer vacation season ended, Chief Fat Bottom's closed down for the winter, and Kristi and I became absorbed in a new, highly-profitable sales program. The church was prospering, and our Christian walk was growing by leaps and bounds. Things could not have been going better for us when we received even more good news. We were blessed to find out that we would be the parents of another baby in early April.

9

No, God, This Just
Can't Be Happening

On January 25, 1985, things took a radical change for the worse. It was a bitterly cold morning, about 5:00 am when we were awakened by a loud pounding on our front door in Kalispell, Montana. I had just gotten back from a sales trip the day before and was sound asleep when the pounding began. It was an unfriendly sound that I had become all too familiar with in my criminal past. I looked at Kristi in horror and exclaimed, "No, God, this just can't be happening! I thought it was all over with." I believed I had dodged a speeding bullet by not having to serve jail time for my drug-dealing past.

We knew the police would bust through the doors any second. Kristi cried, "Tom, we don't have any choice! I have to open it." She ran to open the door, and the police burst through, armed with rifles and pistols.

"We have a warrant for the arrest of Thomas D. Wells for being a narcotics dealer in Milwaukee, Wisconsin," they announced. "Where is Wells?" I walked out of our bedroom with my arms raised, and surrendered. Kristi was terrified, and both she and Tommy began to cry.

We were told that I would be locked up in the Kalispell County jail until I could either post bond or be extradited to Milwaukee. I said good-bye to Kristi and Tommy and told them, "God will get us out of this. You can count on it. He will not let us down. Call Pastor Tom and let him know what's going down. I love you, darling. God will somehow get us out of this mess." After that last statement, the sheriff deputies quickly escorted me to jail where I was booked. The sergeant informed me that I was being held without bail.

"Ever murderers get bail. Why can't I? What am I being held for?"

"The only information I have is that you are wanted for dealing narcotics in Milwaukee, Wisconsin, and that you have also violated your probation and cannot be released," the sergeant answered me.

I was in a state of shock as they led me to my cell. I couldn't believe this was happening. Everything had been going great. We were living for God, and my sinful past was under the Blood of Christ. It had been forgiven and forgotten in God's eyes, however, my past had not been forgiven or Forgotten by the world. I suddenly came to the cold, harsh realization that I had to reap what I had sown in my past. Galatians 6:7 says, *"Be not deceived; God is not mocked; for whatsoever a man soweth, that shall he also reap."*

I knew Kristi and Pastor Tom would come to visit me as soon as they could. I was tremendously concerned for Kristi. She was now six and one-half months pregnant with our second child, and this ordeal wasn't good for her. All I could do was seek the face of God in prayer. I was so uptight that I couldn't even read the Bible.

I was told that fighting extradition would be useless and would only delay things, that Milwaukee would get me anyway. The sergeant explained further, "Officers are flying in to extradite you to face charges in Milwaukee. There is a ten-day extradition period in which they must appear here to take you back, or you will be automatically released."

So many thoughts were racing through my mind that I couldn't think straight. My only desire was to see Kristi and Tommy and to comfort them. Later that day I had visitors, and I was escorted to a protective glass enclosure where I could see my guests and speak to them on the telephone. I was overjoyed to see

Kristi with Tommy sitting on her lap. She picked up the phone, and I said, "Please forgive me, honey. Somehow I will make all of this up to you." She looked so sad and tired. She probably hadn't slept since my arrest. I really didn't know what to tell her, but I spoke up, saying, "God is on our side, and somehow, someway, He will come through for us."

"Tom," she said, "what am I going to do? I can't handle this alone. Tommy is just eighteen months old, and now the baby is due in less than two and one-half months. What am I going to do if you have to go to prison? Oh, God, please help us."

Things could not have been worse for us. It seemed as though the whole world was suddenly caving in all around us. We were rendered powerless, and it looked as though all hope was gone. I knew how the police despised me back in Milwaukee. If they got their hands on me, I was a dead man. I couldn't share that fact with Kristi because if she really knew just how hopeless my case actually was, I thought she might lose the baby. I couldn't be strong only for myself. I knew I had to be strong for us all. I boldly told her, "God has never let me down in the past, even when I wasn't serving Him. He's sure not going to let us down now that we're living for Him. We need to trust Him, no matter what the circumstances look like. God is more powerful than the police, the drug charges, the probation hold, and my past criminal record. All of these things look bad, I know, but God is *greater* than all of them. Kristi, we need to trust in God like never before. If there ever was a time to trust and believe, now is that time." I was convinced in my heart that God would come through, although I didn't know how or when.

"Oh, God," I prayed with Kristi, "please answer our prayer. We need to hear Your voice. Give us a word straight from Heaven so that we can know how to pray. We are so devastated and disillusioned right now that we have no direction on how to pray in this matter. God, please speak a word in season to us who are so oppressed and weary."

Suddenly, a prayer was birthed into my spirit, and I exclaimed, "Kristi, I've got it! God has just given me His direction on how we are to pray. This will be our prayer: We're going to ask the Lord to release me from jail in time for the birth of our baby. I know it seems we're asking for the impossible, but God does the impossible. Jesus said in John 14:13-14, *'And whatsoever you shall ask in my Name, that will I do that the Father may be glorified in the Son. If you shall ask anything in my Name, I will do it.'* This will be our sincere and constant prayer. We will ask, in Jesus' Name, that God would do the absolutely impossible for us. Kristi, will you make a commitment to me that this will be our prayer?"

We finished praying, and a big smile flashed across Kristi's face. The spirit of depression and heaviness over our lives had been broken. Kristi and Tommy left that day filled with the joy of the Lord. I was convinced in my heart that God was going to do something for us that we would never forget.

The next day Pastor Tom came to visit me, and I told him about the specific prayer that Kristi and I had committed to pray in Jesus' Name. He said, "Tom, if that is your prayer, then that will also be the church's prayer from this day forward."

I said, "I love you, Pastor Tom, and I know that God will answer our prayer."

The days flew by quickly, and on every visitor's day, I knew that I could count on Kristi and Tommy being there. We encouraged each other by spending every day reading God's Word and bombarding Heaven's gates with incessant prayer.

A total of eight days had now passed, and there was still no word from the police in Wisconsin. Maybe this would be our miracle. In just two more days, I would be automatically released from jail if the authorities did not come to extradite me.

10

If A Man's Ways Please The Lord

It was early the next morning, about 8:30 am when the sergeant told me the heart-wrenching news.

"Wells, get up! The vice squad from Milwaukee is here."

My heart sank, and I became nauseous and out of breath. I realized that our prayer for getting out of jail wasn't going to be answered at this time.

As the sergeant opened the cell doors, I asked him who had come to get me. He said, "Two high-ranking officers from the vice squad in Milwaukee."

My heart rate and pulse soared when I heard this. I took a deep breath and wiped the sweat off my brow. *No! It can't be the same officers that had vowed to get me. It has got to be someone else,* I thought to myself. *But what if it is them? God, I hope not. They'll kill me! They'll torture me! I'll never make it to the plane alive! They said they'd hunt and gun me down. What are the chances that it could be the same two guys?*

My mind reflected back to that hot, humid summer night in 1982. it was a time in my life when I had become hardened, rebellious, and arrogant because my life was totally permeated with drugs, crime, and sin. I was dealing cocaine like there was no tomorrow. I could sell dump-truck loads of drugs, if I could just get my hands on them. Even with some of the biggest dealers in town supplying all the cocaine I needed for my customers, I would often run out. But things were about to change because of the contacts I was making with major out-of-state sources. Soon all of my suppliers would be buying directly from me, and I would become the drug kingpin in Milwaukee.

One night I had an overwhelming feeling I just couldn't ignore. I somehow knew deep in my spirit that I was under surveillance. No one had spoken to me, but I just knew I was under the scrutinizing eye of a police surveillance team. Cloaked by the darkness of night, I stealthily smuggled my entire cocaine supply out of the house through the backyard and moved it to a secret location. When I returned home, I thoroughly cleaned every crack and crevice, making absolutely sure that I left no traces or signs of cocaine, other than a computer scale and a crack pipe. After making the house arrest-proof, I went out, dealt cocaine, and partied the remainder of the night.

I came home early the next morning, drunk and high. While Kristi was still sleeping, I really got blasted. I began smoking up my cocaine stash, approximately two grams of "rocks" that remained from my night out. As I took my last monstrous hit on the crack pipe, I observed something outside of the picture window that looked like a slow-motion movie. I saw scores of police and unmarked cars surrounding my house. They stormed out of their vehicles toward the front, side, and rear of my home with a battering ram. I was stunned when I heard the frightening sound of their pistols and rifles engaging. They were shouting to one another as they began to smash my front door down. As I ran through the living room into the kitchen, I smashed the pipe against the wall, shattering it into a thousand pieces.

I knew that only seconds remained before the door would be broken down and I would be put under arrest for dealing narcotics, so I decided to pull a brazen trick on the cops. I thought to myself, *This is going to be an absolutely rotten day anyway, so why not get a great laugh out of it?* I knew the coppers wouldn't laugh, but at least the Milwaukee Police Department would have something bizarre to talk about for many years to come.

I knew exactly what I wanted to do. In my refrigerator, I kept a large, plastic gallon container of vitamin C powder, which I would add to my orange juice as a supplement. This vitamin C was very unique because it looked exactly like cocaine. It was gleaming white in color, like mother of pearl, and full of crystals that sparkled just like the best kilo of cocaine one could buy.

With no time to spare, I took the vitamin C and poured it all over my computer scale and mirrors in the pantry where I weighted and cut my cocaine. It looked as though I had a large quantity of pure, glimmering cocaine piled an inch high! Anyone just walking in would be certain that I was a major drug dealer.

I shouted to Kristi that the police were breaking in and went to the front door to greet my unwelcome guests. The door flew open, and the police and vice cops burst into the house with guns pointed at my head. As the hordes of officers poured in, they quickly put me under arrest.

In a typical rebellious display of the obnoxious attitude I had at that time, I blew my last huge hit of cocaine smoke into the vice squad officers' faces and said, "Welcome, fellas. You guys have made a real big mistake this time. what's the charge, you flunky pigs?"

"You are under arrest for major cocaine dealing," they said.

I defiantly laughed in their faces as they slapped the cuffs on me. "There are no drugs here," I said.

The officers quickly responded, "We know that you've got a large quantity of drugs here! You've been under surveillance for over a year, and we know, without question, you have cocaine in this house."

I laughed even louder, saying, "You guys got the wrong man and the wrong house! Like I said, there are no drugs here!"

They began to tear the house apart searching for the drugs. By this time Kristi had come out of the bedroom and was standing in the dining room.

"Hey, show some respect and decency, and let my girl put on her robe. I don't want you cops gawking at her."

Just a couple of minutes had gone by when a short, female vice squad officer came running out of my kitchen, yelling, "We got him! We got him! There's a big pile of cocaine all over the place! It's all over the pantry and all over his scale and mirrors! It's a major bust. We got him, everybody!" I laughed so loud, I thought I woke up the neighbors across the street.

One of the head cops shouted, "Shut up! What are you laughing about? If I were in your shoes, I wouldn't be laughing You're going to jail today, funny man."

"That's not cocaine!" I said defiantly.

"Yes, it is," they said. "It's all over the kitchen. didn't you hear what she said?"

"I'm sorry to disappoint you, gentlemen, but what you see in the kitchen and all over the pantry is not cocaine."

They asked, jeering at me, "Then what would you call that sparkling, white substance?"

"Oh, *that* sparkling, white substance!" I said sarcastically. You mean that shiny, white substance in the kitchen? Oh, that is vitamin C."

"Yeah, right, vitamin C!" they mocked.

"No, it really is vitamin C," I mused. "You see, I put a little scoop of it in my orange juice to keep in good health. If you don't believe me, the large plastic container on the floor will verify that I'm telling the truth. Besides, it's a law that you must immediately do a drug test on the scene to determine whether something is illegal or not, right?"

One of the officers picked up the plastic bottle and brought it to the arresting officer. "Is this the bottle you're talking about?" he asked me.

"Yep, that's the one. As you can see, there's still some vitamin C in the bottom of it, and if you read the label, it will tell you that it is exactly what I said it is."

The officer looked inside the bottle, read the label, and said,

"He's right. We need to test this stuff and see if it is cocaine or not."

Some of the other officers responded, "No way. This guy's lying! This stuff looks just like cocaine. It's got to be cocaine."

They began to test the crystal-white substance, and in a few moments, they would know for sure. I knew I had them in a very humiliating position. I also knew that cocaine, when it is tested properly with the special police testing equipment, will turn a bright, royal blue. I had tested cocaine many times in the past with virtually the same testing equipment and knew the color it had to turn to test positive. As the test was being completed, I could tell the vice squad detectives were under tremendous pressure to make this bust a success.

When the test was complete, the color of the chemicals turned into a pale pink. The cop who did the testing spoke up, saying, "What in the world *is* this stuff"

I chuckled and said, "I told you, it's vitamin C. I put one little scooper-dooper of this in a quart of orange juice every day, and it gives me all the vitamin C that I need to keep my body healthy, strong, and vibrant for the busy, hectic lifestyle I keep."

All of the vice squad officers' faces turned beet red with embarrassment and anger when they realized that they had been duped and that they had made a very serious blunder.

There were approximately fifty police officers in and around my house for what they thought would be a major drug bust. The leader of the uniformed officers involved in the bust shouted out to the vice squad officers, "This is the biggest blunder you guys have ever pulled off! This guy had the coke right here in the house last night, and somehow he got it right out from under your noses! You had this slime-ball-puke under surveillance for over a year – you had him dead in the water – and still, he got the coke out of the house without you even knowing about it! You guys are a disgrace to your uniforms!"

"Yeah, you're right! You guys are a disgrace to your uniforms! I yelled.

For a moment, even I felt sorry for those poor, sad, pathetic coppers. Those guys really were a disgrace to the force. I wanted to crack a joke at that time, but I wasn't stupid. I knew just how far to go with this gag, and I knew I had gone far enough.

There was a deafening silence in the house. These cops, and many others, had spent years trying to bust this Las Vegas playboy. No doubt, tens of thousands of dollars of taxpayers' money had been wasted on this bungled fiasco. They could have easily walked in my house hundreds of times and caught me red-handed, but the one time they go for the big bust, they come up empty-handed with mud on their faces. I thought to myself, *Well, tough luck, fellas. Better luck next time, Jose!*

Kristi then pointed out to them, "Even if you had found drugs, they would belong to me. This house is in my name, and Tom is my guest from Vegas." The cops just shook their heads in utter disgust.

Just then, the same short, female copper came running out of the kitchen again and said, "No we got him! We can arrest him! We can send him to jail!"

I yelled out in disbelief, "For what? What's the charge now?"

She held up one of my books and said, "This is it! I have it right here in my hands: an overdue library book. You are under arrest for an overdue library book!"

I couldn't believe my ears, and judging by the looks on the officers' faces, I don't think they could believe their ears, either! Laughing, I threw up my hands and said, "I'm guilty! I'm guilty! Take me in. I surrender. You're right, I'm guilty of possessing an overdue library book!"

The cops were all looking at one another, asking, "Can we arrest him for that? No way, we better not. We look bad enough as it is. We don't want to look any more foolish than we already do."

One of the vice squad leaders, a detective named Wilke, took me into the kitchen. "Sit down, Wells, and get that stupid smirk off your face! I don't know how you did it – how you got the coke out – and I don't really give a damn. But let me tell you this: I'll get

49

you! One day you will make a mistake, and I will be there to gun you down. Do you hear what I'm saying? Whenever you look over your shoulder, watch for me. One day I will be there. I will be there if I have to chase you and hunt you down halfway around the world. You are mine! Do you understand me, Mr. Wells, Mr. Vegas Hotshot? If you will confess your guilt by admitting to us that you are a cocaine dealer and telling us who your suppliers are, we will give you a break and offer you a deal. If not, we are going to haul you and your pretty girlfriend off to jail. So, what's your answer?"

"I've got an answer for you! You Milwaukee cops are fools, the biggest morons in the country," I laughed. "I don't know where you guys got your police training – probably somewhere in a barnyard or a watermelon patch way out in the sticks – but let me tell you something: You, Mr. Pig, are a joke, and on your best day you will never catch me on my worst day. Do you understand? I know my rights. Either arrest me for an overdue library book or get out of this house. If not, I will have *you* arrested for trespassing and police harassment! Do you understand me, Mr. Wilke, Mr. Vice Squad Hotshot? Never forget what I said: You will never catch me. I'm way too smart for you."

Wilke shot back, "You think you got one over on us pretty good today with the phony-baloney cocaine and all the jokes and laughs, but remember, someday you will be mine. Mark my words! You will be mine!"

Those vicious threats of detective Wilke, spoken only a few years earlier, were still echoing in my mind as I was escorted out of my cell to the entrance of the booking room where I would meet my awaiting captors. I prayed nervously, *Lord, if ever You hear me, please hear me today. I have only one request. Please don't let them be Wilke and Pearson, the two cops that vowed to get me.*

I walked into the booking room and couldn't believe my eyes. There they were, Wilke and Pearson, my worst enemies! I could see the burning hatred in their eyes and the immense satisfaction they were experiencing. Wilke spoke up, grinning "There's our man! Wells, we told you we'd get you. We got you now, and you belong to us."

I was speechless and knew I was in for some big trouble. They slapped the cuffs and shackles on so tightly that I began to lose feeling in my hands and feet. They started roughing me up, yanking and jerking on the cuffs, yelling, "Wells, we are going to slam-dunk you. You're ours now!"

"Listen," I said. "I've got something to say. I've got something to tell you."

"Shut up, Wells!" they shot back. "As far as we're concerned, you have nothing to say to us. Must we remind you about when you had the smart mouth back in Milwaukee?"

I looked at the sergeant from the Kalispell jail and asked him, "Sergeant, can I please call my wife and say good-bye?"

Pearson interrupted, "Absolutely not! No calls for this man. He is extremely dangerous, and we're afraid that he may have planned a breakout."

"I have no intention of trying to break out," I said. "I just want to say good-bye to my wife and son. She's seven months pregnant and would be crushed if I didn't call her before I leave."

"Wells, shut up! We don't care about your stories or your wife. The plane is leaving in half an hour, and we'll be there on time with no problems from you. Do I make myself clear?!

"Yes sir, you do."

I realized these men were hardened toward me and would not budge for a moment to listen to anything I had to say. I would be better off just keeping my mouth shut. They led me out the front door into a waiting sheriff's car that would take us to the airport. I was devastated that I couldn't say good-bye to my wife and son, and I knew that Kristi would be heartbroken. But I was powerless; there was nothing I could do.

As we drove to the airport, they began to tell me, "Wells, this time we got you! You're not under arrest for some phony cocaine or for an overdue library book. This time we're throwing the book at you. You're facing twelve years in prison for two counts of delivery of cocaine to an undercover police officer. You also violated your probation by leaving the state. With your prior record, we are going to put you away for a long, long time, Mr. Vegas Pretty Boy. We have information that tells us you've brought your organization here to escape the investigation by the Feds and that you're currently working with some of the largest drug cartels in the nation.

"Well, we've spoiled your grandiose plans, and we will do everything in our power to make sure you never see the light of day again. But if you tell us who your main drug suppliers are, we will consider the possibility of taking a few years off your sentence. If you decide not to cooperate with us, we will make sure you spend the whole twelve years in prison, with no possibility of parole. The courts in Milwaukee have known for some time that you've been a major dealer for years, and they will be happy to bring you to swift justice. Do you understand me?"

I knew these cops were lying. They didn't really have any information on me. If someone had been watching me recently, they would have known of my wholehearted commitment to Jesus Christ. And if I was truly under surveillance, they would have surely seen me going to church four times a week and working regular jobs trying to earn a clean and honest living.

I finally said, "Men, I do have something to tell you, but I know it's not what you want to hear. I'm not a drug dealer anymore. I'm married now and have one son and another child on the way. I'm working a regular job, and I didn't move to Montana to use or deal drugs. I moved here to get away from the drugs and the dealers. I can honestly say I don't know anyone who deals drugs out here, and if I did, I wouldn't have anything to do with them. All I ask is that you give me a few minutes, and I will tell you everything."

"Shut up, Wells!" they yelled. "We've had enough of your lies. We know that you've moved your headquarters from Vegas and Milwaukee to Montana. We know this for a fact, and there is nothing that you can say that will persuade us otherwise. Wells, you and other scumbags like you will never change. You're dealers, junkies, and heartless killers. Nothing in this world could ever change people like you. Now listen, this is your last chance.

Either tell us who your connections are, or go to prison for the rest of your life."

I said, "Officers, if you would let me explain, I could tell you something that would make a difference."

"Wells, if you have something to say, tell us who your people are."

"I'm trying to explain that I don't have any people, and I'm not involved in drugs, or anything like that anymore!" I exclaimed. "I have changed."

"Shut up, Wells!" they retorted. "We don't want to hear another word about your life. We know that you're still dealing drugs, and unless you give us the names of your connections and associates, we don't have anything more to talk about. Do you understand English, or must we write it out for you? We don't want to hear any excuses, problems, stories, fairy tales, or anything else you have on your mind. All we want are names of your people and contacts. Then we will listen."

"I told you, men, I nave no people or contacts to give you. I'm no longer a drug dealer, and I have no involvement in those things anymore. If you would give me a chance, I will explain."

"All right, Wells, we've had enough!" one of the officers said harshly. "I'm not going to say this again, and I'm not slurring my works! This is your last chance. Either give us your people or don't say another word!"

As he made that last threatening statement, we arrived at the Kalispell Airport. The plane was departing in fifteen minutes, and as we approached the gate, I felt ashamed and embarrassed to be seen handcuffed and shackled in leg irons, with the vice squad officers gripping my arms. But the Lord reminded me that although I looked liked a desperate criminal in the eyes of the world, I was truly a child of the King. I felt the love of Jesus burning deep within my heart. I was bound and headed for prison, but I knew I belonged to Christ and that I was actually a free man.

Suddenly, I stopped dead in my tracks when I saw Kristi and Tommy out of the corner of my eye. They were running toward me. I turned around, and there they were, right in front of me. I looked at Wilke and Pearson and said, "Men, this is my wife and little boy, Tommy. Would you please allow me to say good-bye to them?" When the officers saw my pregnant wife and little boy standing there weeping, they realized that what I had told them about my family was true.

"Okay, Wells, you can say good-bye, but just for a few minutes because we have a plane to catch. First, we have to search her for any weapons."

After the search, Kristi, Tommy, and I hugged like there was no tomorrow. No words were spoken, just a deep love given to one another. Words couldn't express the great pain and sorrow we were experiencing as we separated, not knowing if or when we would see one another again. Then I asked Kristi, "How did you know that I was leaving? They wouldn't let me call you because they thought I would try to escape."

She said, "Tom, it was a miracle! The sergeant from Kalispell called me up just fifteen minutes ago and said, 'Kristi, this is the sergeant from the jail. Tom has just been picked up by the vice squad and is now being transported back to Milwaukee. If you hurry, you might be able to see him before he gets on that plane. And please, don't say I called you, because I could lose my job.'"

When I heard this, I prayed, *Oh thank you, thank you Jesus, for allowing us to say good-bye to one another. Lord, bless that sergeant for his act of compassion upon us. Watch over my family as we depart this day, and God, please answer our prayer that I will be released from jail for the birth of our baby. Amen.*

"Kristi, I love you and Tommy. And remember, God will do the impossible for us. Good-bye, my love."

Wilke grabbed me by the arm, and I waved good-bye as we entered the jet. I was taken to the very rear of the plane and seated at a window seat with Wilke and Pearson to my left. The plane departed for Milwaukee but first made a couple of minor stops in Montana. After we boarded the plane, neither of my escorts said a word to me until Pearson unexpectedly spoke up. "Wells, you made the comment in the car that you had something you wanted to say to us. Well, I'd like to hear what you have to say."

Wilke agreed, saying, "Yeah, Wells, I would also like to hear what you've got to say."

I was shocked that they were actually giving me an opportunity to talk. There was no question in my mind that they despised me. To them, I was nothing but an arrogant, worthless thug, an incorrigible junkie and drug dealer. Their only intention was to put me away for life.

At first, I didn't know what to say and asked the Lord to give me the right words – words that would speak to their hearts so that they would believe I was no longer their worst enemy, but a Christian who loved people and Jesus Christ. I measured my words carefully as I began to speak. For the next few minutes, I was able to share with them how Jesus had miraculously changed my life and made me a totally new and different person.

I began by saying, "Thanks for giving me this opportunity. You men have come a long way to arrest me, and if I am found guilty, I'll go to prison for twelve years. For those charges, I am totally guilty, but I am actually guilty of much, much more. You see, if the truth were known, I could be be sent to prison for many thousands of years. For many years I have been a dealer of not only cocaine, but also marijuana, heroin, and other drugs. I was a bookmaker, and I gambled illegally. I committed an armed robbery when I was twenty. I've been a "player" and consorted with pimps and prostitutes. I even kidnapped two men who ripped me off. I've never killed anyone, but I came as close to killing as any man could. I've stolen, cheated, lied, and done many other horrible things. I am deeply ashamed for all of these crimes. I was guilty before both God and man for being a wretched drug dealer."

Tears began to pour down my face as I asked the officers, "Mr. Wilke and Mr. Pearson, I beg of you, would you forgive me for what I have done to you and for being a drug dealer in Milwaukee? Would you please forgive me for hurting and destroying countless lives?" Just over two years ago, I had fallen as hopelessly far away from God as any man ever could. The fiendish, demonic stronghold of cocaine, heroin, and alcohol had me in a tenacious death grip, and I was virtually a dead man. I was consumed by lust, money, power, and greed, and I would have stopped at nothing to accomplish my selfish goals. I was a fugitive from the Lord and had come to a place of utter ruin, even to a point *beyond* suicide. I had known and loved Jesus Christ all of my life, but I departed from him when I was just fifteen years old.

When I was twenty-eight, God said to me, *"Tom, there is no hope for you, no hope! You have trampled upon the Blood of My Son!"* I begged God to give me one more chance to live. I repented of my sins and asked God for forgiveness and told Him I would serve Him all the days of my life. With all hope gone and my life slipping away, Jesus came and rescued me from destruction. He washed my vile sins away and gave my life back to me.

"Kristi and I moved away from Milwaukee to Montana to begin our lives over again and live for Jesus Christ with all of our hearts. This is my story. it's the honest truth. Kristi, our little boy, and I are a living testimony of the saving and life-changing power that is in the Name and Blood of Jesus Christ."

I looked into the eyes of those two tough vice squad detectives and saw that their eyes were filled with tears. I could see that in only a matter of minutes, God had super-naturally intervened on my behalf and touched their hearts through my sincere testimony. He miraculously changed their attitude toward me, from one of total hostility to one of compassion. We all were totally awestruck at the complete transformation that had just taken place in our hearts.

They said, "Tom, when we heard about your arrest, we couldn't wait to get our hands on you. We considered you to be our worst enemy, and our only desire was to put you in prison and throw away the key. But after what you have just told us, we have changed our minds about you and want to become your friends. We believe that you truly have changed and forgive you for being a dealer and for the things that you did to us in the past. We are even willing to make a commitment to help you with your case in any way we can."

When I heard them say this, I found it hard to believe that I was talking to the same two men that had their hearts set on revenge only a short time before.

They said, "When we get back to Milwaukee, we'll try to get bail set for you, but it won't be easy. As you know, the authorities think that you purposely fled to avoid prosecution on these charges. In addition, you're on a probation hold with Mr. Jones, your probation officer, and we have no authority over a probation hold. But we will do all that we can to help you. Remember what we said: We are now your friends, and we promise to stand by your side to the end." Then Wilke and Pearson held out their hands to shake on our new friendship.

Oh, the goodness, greatness, and magnificence of our God! Proverbs 16:7 says, *"When a man's ways please the Lord, He maketh even his enemies to be at peace with him."*

During the remainder of the flight, I praised and worshiped God for His tender mercies and the great miracle He had just performed. I was ecstatic and couldn't wait to tell Kristi how God had so quickly and powerfully softened the vice squad officers' hearts.

Before our plane had even left the state of Montana, my enemies had become my friends. We laughed and joked around together just as if we were old friends and talked about our families and precious moments in our lives. I even mentioned my dream of one day opening a family-owned pizzeria, and they loved the idea. Wilke even quipped he might make an investment in it. Man, we serve a truly awesome God!

11

Salvations In The
House Of Correction

It was sundown on February 1st when our plane touched down at Mitchell Field in shivering-cold Milwaukee, Wisconsin. From there we went straight to the Milwaukee County Jail where I was held without bail until my first court arraignment.

My arrival into Milwaukee had come on the wave of a wondrous miracle from God. Being an eyewitness to how the Lord moved so dramatically to give me favor in the hearts of my former enemies was mind-boggling. Only God could do that. It made me think of the countless people who have been so powerfully changed over the centuries by the lives and testimonies of Jesus' faithful disciples while they were in chains for their testimony of Christ. The Apostles Paul, Silas, and Peter, as well as John the Baptist, serve as Biblical examples of this.

Instead of returning to my hometown discouraged because of my arrest and separation from my family, I was joyful and filled with anticipation because I knew God was doing something I would never forget.

Pearson and Wilke booked me and then told me, "Tom, tomorrow we'll find out just where you stand and if bail can be granted in your case. Remember, you're facing some pretty stiff odds right now, and you need to be patient. By all means, please stay out of trouble while you are in here. Don't forget, we've committed ourselves to helping you, and we'll see you again in the next few days."

When I appeared in court the next morning, I quickly found out exactly where I stood. No bail would be granted for either of my cases. The judge and the district attorney (D.A.) were adamant in their belief that I had fled Wisconsin to avoid prosecution on the cocaine charges. It would be difficult to persuade them otherwise.

The probation violation case was a totally different matter. Larry Jones was my probation officer (P.O.) in this case, and the judge had no authority in regard to setting bail. At present, I was on a probation hold, and the only person who could lift that hold was Mr. Jones. The judge also appointed an attorney for me because I couldn't afford one. After my court hearing, I was brought back to my cell and given my first opportunity to make a telephone call.

Although my first day in court was somewhat discouraging, my confidence in the Lord was still strong. I called Kristi and shared the unbelievable report of how God had moved in my life and in the hearts of Wilke and Pearson during the plane flight. She rejoiced that my one-time enemies were now going to bat for me by trying to help me obtain my release on bail. I told her court didn't go well that day, but that I had another appearance in two weeks, and we needed to stay encouraged.

My son Tommy came on the line and said, "Daddy, I love you. Mommy and I are praying for you."

I told them both, "Keep on praying because God is on the move."

The next day I was pleasantly surprised that Wilke and Pearson came to see me. "Tom, we've done all that we can. Nothing more can be done about your bail, primarily because of your probation officer. He's the key for any hope of an early release. We want to let you know we're looking out for you and will come to visit whenever we can." I told them that jail time wasn't easy time, but that my hopes were high that I would be released on bail after I talked with Larry Jones. After they left, I thanked the Lord for giving me these new friends, and I told Him I would try to be a good Christian example to them.

The days passed slowly while I waited for Jones to show up at the jail to meet with me. I couldn't understand what the holdup was or why he was taking so long to come. I knew it was mandatory for him to visit me within fourteen days of my booking, and I was anxious to see him.

After spending eight days in the county jail, I was transferred to the House of Correction (H.O.C.) located in Franklin, Wisconsin. This prison facility housed hundreds of men who were either serving time or awaiting trial on various charges. Some were imprisoned for minor offenses, such as driving suspensions and revocations. Others were in for delinquency in child support payment, and still others were in for more serious offenses, such as armed robbery, molestation, and rape. I had served time in this bastille before and was all too familiar with this escape-proof little "Sing Sing," but now I came back as a servant of the Most High God.

In the H.O.C. I encountered men that I knew from my former life of sin and drug dealing. One of them was motorcycle gang leader, Dick the Beard. On the streets these men were considered "major movers." they all were astonished to find out that "Tom the Player" had become "Tom the Preacher." I ministered the love of Christ to them, and God began to work marvelously in their lives.

My first two weeks in the H.O.C. seemed to drag by endlessly, and I was excited when the day for my first formal court hearing arrived. I was also scheduled to see my probation officer on the same day. I was anxiously looking forward to my first meeting with him and had great expectations about the possibility of being released that day.

When Jones saw me, he glared at me and said, "Well, look who's here, Mr. Wells, the cocaine dealer." I knew I was in big trouble then. "I've been looking forward to seeing you," he said smugly. "I'm an extremely busy man, and I'm going to make this meeting as brief as possible. I have many other cases that are much more important than yours, and quite frankly, I don't give a damn about you or your case. As far as I'm concerned, you fled from the state to avoid prosecution on these new drug charges, and there's nothing that you can say to change my mind."

"In regard to your earlier probation case for the criminal damage of property, I have you on a probation hold, and I have no intention of releasing you. I have total authority over you, and there's no one but me that can relinquish that hold – not a judge, not an attorney, not even your vice squad pals. I've already discussed your case with them, and quite frankly, it's a joke.

He sneered sadistically at me and said, "You see, Wells, I don't give a damn about your so-called conversion to Jesus or your born-again experience, if that's what you call it. I don't give a damn about your pregnant wife and child back in Montana, and I really don't give a damn about these stupid, ignorant cops that you've somehow duped into being on your side.

"Let me tell you why. As far as I'm concerned, you're vomit, a low-life, good-for-nothing drug merchant, and now you belong to me. According to state law, I can hold you for one year." I looked at him incredulously. He sneered again and said, "Yeah, that's right, one whole year. And in that time you will be found guilty of these new drug charges, and you will – I can assure you – be put behind bars for quite a long time; hopefully, the whole twelve years."

"Now, to make certain that we have no misunderstanding here, it's like I said, you're mine, and I am going to hold you for one year. You get my drift, Mr. Drug Pusher?"

I pleaded, "But Larry, if you would just give me a minute, I could explain..."

He quickly interrupted, "Could it be that you are more stupid than you look? I told you, man, we have nothing to talk about. Absolutely nothing. Now, I'm leaving, and I don't want to hear another word out of your mouth. Do I make myself perfectly clear, Mr. Wells?'

All I could say was, "Yes, Mr. Jones, you do."

"Woe is me! Woe is me!" is all I could utter to myself after he left. I now more fully understood how the Prophet Jeremiah felt when he was not only cast into the dungeon, but dropped into the muck of the miry pit as well. If the devil himself had met with me,

I think I would have stood a better chance. At least with the devil, I could have bound and rebuked him "in the Name of Jesus" and cast him someplace, anyplace. But this guy was totally unreasonable, and his heart was thoroughly hardened toward me. I expected Wilke and Pearson to act that way toward me, but not Larry Jones. It would take a miracle similar to the parting of the Red Sea for God to reach Jones.

I felt totally beaten down and deflated as I left my meeting with him. I mean, if I could have talked, I wouldn't have wanted to. This problem was much bigger than I had imagined. I knew it *looked* hopeless before, but now it *was* hopeless. I needed desperately to get back to the H.O.C. and earnestly pray about this. I had hoped and prayed for the best, but with this deceived and thoroughly biased probation authority holding me, I had little hope.

I finally came to the realization that my hope wasn't in Larry Jones or the justice system or even in Wilke and Pearson. My hope was in nothing less than Jesus Christ and His righteousness. I had to put my trust in Christ and in Him alone. If all my hope was placed only in Him, then no matter what the circumstances looked like, I would still be *"more than a conqueror"* through Him who loved me.

I called Kristi and told her that my case was being delayed because of manifold complications but that God was still in charge, and He was going to come through for us. I didn't feel led to break the saddening news to her about my awful meeting with Mr. Jones. I needed to protect her and the baby from any unnecessary trauma.

After the confrontation with Jones and the much-needed time alone with God, I made a firm decision that no matter what Jones, the justice system, or even the devil himself had planned to do with me, I was going to serve the Lord with all of my heart and strength and win many souls to Christ.

I began this mission by starting a men's prayer meeting in the H.O.C. chapel. At first, I couldn't get any cooperation from Dave Sorenson, the head chaplain. I had asked him repeatedly for permission to schedule a time for prayer with other inmates, but was denied each time. I continued to ask, seek, and knock until, I believe, I finally wore out this soft-spoken, loving man. He granted my request, and rapidly, God began to work in the men's lives.

I began attending the various Christian church services that were held at the H.O.C. and became friends with the men and women of God who came to minister to our needs every week. Among them were Mark and Pam Jefferson and their sidekick, Hank. Through their anointed preaching and singing ministry, many other prisoners and I were strengthened and uplifted. Pam often called my wife and encouraged her faith, and they would spiritually link arms with us to pray, in Jesus' Name, for my release from jail.

After two more weeks had passed, I went to my second scheduled court appearance, this time with a new court-appointed attorney. The judge denied bail on both of my cases, and again my hearing was postponed for two more weeks. I had now been in jail for thirty-six days, and absolutely nothing had been accomplished. In addition, my new attorney told me that he also was being removed from my case and that another lawyer would be appointed.

I found the justice system to be terribly corrupt, contemptible, disorganized, and downright frustrating. After this last adjournment, another abandonment by an attorney, and no further word from Larry Jones, I knew that my faith was being severely tested. All I could do was believe God's Word which says in Ephesians 6:13-14, *"Wherefore take unto you the whole armor of God, that you may be able to withstand in the evil day, and having done all to stand. Stand!"* The evil day had come violently upon my life, and in the midst of this debauchery, I had made the decision to stand! And that's exactly what I was determined to do.

My wife and I continued to press the battle in prayer, and I knew in my spirit that we were gaining significant ground. Although nothing was taking place that we could see in the natural realm regarding my criminal cases, much was taking place in the spiritual realm.

Some formerly incorrigible prisoners were finding new hope as I was able to minister to them in the H.O.C. They were beginning to realize that Christ was their answer. I was also privileged to be given a much sought-after job working in the canteen-commissary. My friendship with Dick the Beard and his trusted relationship with the canteen manager secured this coveted position for me. This job enabled me to move freely throughout the H.O.C. facility and visit prisoners in the numerous segregated dormitories.

Dick and I had a strong relationship, first in the world as sinners and now in the heavenlies *"seated with Christ."* My leading him to Christ made my entire jail experience well-worth suffering. But there were others who also found forgiveness and peace through the Blood of the Lamb. Dick and many others had been wicked sinners following the ways of the world, but now they were loving saints who *"...looked for a city which hath foundations, whose builder and maker is God"* (Hebrews 11:10), and all the powers in hell couldn't stop their appointment as citizens in that heavenly city.

12

God's Appointed Attorney

After a month had passed, I finally received some positive news. God had answered my prayer for legal help, and my new attorney came to visit me for the first time. I was escorted to a room in which we could have a private conversation.

I was surprised to find that my new legal representative was a woman. I could see a sensitivity in her soft eyes that few people possess. She was attractive, well-dressed, and very articulate. I gladly and warmly welcomed her.

She said, in a very businesslike demeanor, "Tom, my name is Sandy Stone Ruffalo. I've taken on your case, and I see that you've lost two attorneys in the last month. I know you must have been disappointed by that, but I can assure you that won't happen again. Once I start a case, I see it through to the end, and I promise you that I will do the best job that I can."

She continued, "Now that we've met, let's get to know each other better. In the next fifteen minutes or so, could you tell me about your life and about your family in Montana? I take a sincere interest in the lives of all my clients, and your case is very unusual. I want to know everything about you, your wife, and little boy. I want to hear about your dreams and aspirations in life and about how in the world you got yourself in such a predicament as this.

"I've read in your file that you've been extradited from Kalispell for two counts of delivery of cocaine, and you're also on probation hold. Tom, you need to tell me the truth because I need to get a feel for this case. From what I can see, it looks as though the vice squad has an open-and-shut case against you, as far as the charges are concerned. But in my time as a lawyer, I've seen many strange things occur."

I poured my heart out to this "angel of justice" by sharing my life story and telling her about my sincere conversion to Christ. I told her about the vice squad officers' hostility toward me and how, through a miracle of God, they became my friends on the plane ride. I told her how my wife and I and others were believing God for my release from jail for the birth of our baby.

I admitted that I was completely guilty of all charges against me. I told her how God had taken me, a filthy reprobate, and made me a "prince," a "priest," and a "king," according to His promises in the Bible. I told her about Larry Jones and the hatred he exhibited toward me and the probation hold that he would not relinquish. Finally, I spoke of my goal to live a godly, holy life, giving my all to Jesus who gave His all for me.

She listened to me very intently. When I had finished talking, she responded. "Tom, in all of my years as an attorney and an assistant district attorney, I've heard every story and line in the book – and out of the book, for that matter – but I've never heard a story like yours. I feel honored to take your case, and I'm going to do something today that I've never done before. You see, I represent many indigent clients like you who can't afford proper counsel. My legal services for your case are being paid by the state, but after hearing what you've just told me I won't take a dime from them for your case.

"I will represent you at no charge and will defend you as though you were my only son. I'm going to get you a fair trial, and not only that, I'm also going to believe with you that you will be released from jail in time for the birth of your child."

I knew then, in my heart, that the Lord had inspired her to provide the help that I so desperately needed. Sandy was truly "God's appointed attorney."

She looked at me and said, "Tom, we have got our work cut out for us. This is what we're going to do: First, here is my card; call me any time you need to talk. Second, I would like to call Kristi and assure her that you have an attorney who is fighting for both of you. Third, I will personally contact this Mr. Jones and show him the error of his way. And finally, I'll need the names of the vice cops that have befriended you because I need to contact them. To have your arresting officers on our side is perhaps the greatest miracle I have ever heard. Tom, take heart. The battle begins today, and we will see the victory."

After the meeting with Sandy, I couldn't believe what was happening. God's provision through her was almost too good to believe, and I couldn't thank Him enough. I called Kristi and told her to expect a call from our new attorney who had been truly appointed by God. She was glad to hear the glowing reports of all that God was doing. Kristi reminded me that now she was over seven and one-half months pregnant and that if I was going to get home in time, I had better hurry.

Two more weeks had passed since my first meeting with Sandy, and now I was scheduled to go to court again, but this time it would be with an attorney that knew how to fight. In court Sandy rallied in my behalf in front of the judge, trying to persuade her that I did not have any prior knowledge of the cocaine charges and that I had moved to Montana to raise my family in a wholesome environment. Although Sandy was convincing and the best "Perry Mason" I had ever seen, she couldn't convince the judge or the D.A. to grant any bail for me. My case was again postponed for two more weeks, and I left the courtroom very disappointed. But after the hearing, Sandy reminded me, "Tom, you can't allow yourself to get discouraged. This was only my first crack at this judge, and we'll give it our best shot next time out. By the way, I had a great conversation with Kristi. Her spirits are still high, and Tommy's doing just fine. I also spoke with Wilke and Pearson, and they're totally sold out for your cause. They will do anything within their power to help you.

"Tom, God really did work a miracle in that situation. Wilke told me how you smarted off to him the morning of the drug bust.

You sure were quite a character!" she laughed. "I heard about the phony cocaine and that library book story. that's just too much to believe! Are you sure you're the same man that pulled all those shenanigans?"

I said, "Sandy, I can assure you, I am the same man, though different in every way. In 2 Corinthians 5:17 God says, '*Therefore if any man be in Christ, he is a new creature, old things are passed away, behold all things are become new.*' When a person comes to Christ, he becomes a new creation, a totally new creature; old things have passed away, and everything has become new. Sandy, in God's eyes I am a new man, even thought I look the same. I've got the Holy Spirit in my heart."

"Tom, that's amazing!" she said. "Your life has changed tremendously, and I'm grateful to have a small part in it. Before I forget, I wanted to let you know that I have tried to contact Larry Jones's office, but I haven't been able to talk to him. He's avoiding me and hasn't returned any of my calls. It looks as if we're not going to get any help from him at all. I'm going to stop by his office next week so keep up the good work, and we'll get you out of here in no time."

After my appearance in court with Sandy, I realized what a vast difference it made to have an attorney that really believed in my cause. But I also knew that the judges in my cases already had their minds set and were not going to be easily swayed. I had spent over fifty days in the slammer now and was feeling pretty uptight about my time situation. Kristi and Tommy were well, and she was experiencing a healthy pregnancy. However, she was now more than eight months pregnant, so time was getting short.

During my first two months at the H.O.C. I had the aggravating experience of being unnecessarily awakened very early in the morning by the dorm sergeant on two separate occasions. I was told to get up because I was supposedly scheduled to appear in court that day, according to his records. Both times I thought that it was probably a computer error, but I got up and showered anyway and took the early morning prison bus to the county jail. All day long I sat in the cramped bull pen, waiting to be called to court, but the call never came. Inmates are occasionally victims of this kind of mistake.

A whole day in the bull pen at the country jail is no picnic in the park. We were packed in like sardines, and it was the filthiest jail I had ever seen. I had to sit on the floor because of inadequate seating. This place stunk with filth and profanity, and the floor was covered with urine, cigarette butts, and dirty toilet paper. It was despicable in every way. The toilets were stopped up and gave off an odor that was difficult to survive. I endured this situation twice, but I vowed I would never go to court again unless I was certain it was my scheduled date to appear.

13

Little Miracles
From The Lord

Now that I was imprisoned, Kristi couldn't afford to continue paying the rent on our apartment by herself, so she rented a room from a dear friend named Bea Ellen, an old saint who was a member of our church in Montana. It was very hard on Kristi to lose our nice home and have to put our furniture in storage. Being more than eight months pregnant, all alone, and so far from home was a very trying experience for her. I was in a Milwaukee jail over 2,000 miles away, and all of our family and loved ones were also back in Wisconsin.

I will never forget the night I called Kristi and heard the excitement in her voice when she said, "Tom, Bea Ellen and I were in prayer that the Lord would somehow intervene in our circumstance when the Holy Spirit moved upon her. She jumped up joyfully exclaiming, 'It's done, Kristi! It's done in Jesus' Name!' I asked her what she meant, and she said, 'Your prayer for Tom, that he would be set free from jail to be with you. I saw it clear as day, a vision from the Lord. He showed me Tom getting out of jail, and he was with you and the new baby. Oh, Kristi, God has done it. He will answer all our prayers. He has honored your and Tom's steadfast faith!'" what joy I experienced in hearing that word of confirmation straight from my wife's lips!

Another time Kristi mentioned to me that she had seen a small trailer home that was available. She needed exactly three hundred dollars to rent it for us, but since she had no money at all, she asked me to pray that God would bring in the finances we needed. When I called just a few days later to see how she and Tommy were doing, she said, "Tom, God provided the money for our trailer! I called Pastor Rodgers in Milwaukee and told him about the situation. He said he would make our need known to the church congregation and would believe with us that God would provide an answer. Tom, he called back the next day and said the church came up with exactly the amount of money that was needed! Pastor Rodgers and his wife are the kindest people I've ever known. The Lord is so great and wonderful! There isn't anyone like Him in all the earth."

Pastor Rodgers was a pastor's pastor and a man after God's own heart. His faithfulness in the Milwaukee area had given him a reputation as a man of great compassion. Other members of my family had belonged to his church, and he had a great affection for my Grandmother Redlich. Although Grandpa Redlich had passed away years earlier, she continued to press on in the things of God. Now in her eighties, she still went to church whenever the doors were open and was always fervent for the work of the Lord.

Pastor Rodgers came to visit me often in the H.O.C. I appreciated his tenderness toward Kristi and me now during our trying ordeal. Many ministers shrink from the more weighty issues and really difficult problems, but this man embraced our burden and made it his own. For that, I will never forget him.

14

Blessed Is The Man
That Endures
Temptation

When my next court date arrived, Sandy battled for me like a true Spartan once again. If I didn't know any better and still were a betting man, I would have bet my last dollar that she was part Doberman Pinscher. But once again, we were soundly defeated and bail was not granted for the drug charges. It was beginning to dawn on Sandy just how difficult this case actually was.

She was finally able to talk with Larry Jones. Although he wasn't as rude and obnoxious to her as he had been to me, he made it quite clear to her that he was not going to budge an inch – not for her, the vice squad, or even his own mother. Larry told her firmly, "Mr. Wells belongs to me, and you can't have him."

When Sandy told me about her meeting with Larry Jones, she shook her head and threw her hands up in frustration. "Tom, I've done all that I can," she said. "I've never encountered such a difficult probation officer. If there ever was a couple who deserved a break, I believe it's you and Kristi. You've both come a long way, and I want to see you through this thing. We're not giving up by any means, but unless Jones has a thorough heart and attitude change, there's little that can be done. It's a little late in the game now, but perhaps we can request a change of probation officers."

I had now spent sixty-nine straight days in jail and had never been so frustrated in all my life. At times, I honestly considered pulling a jailbreak. The justice system is so unfair and corrupt, I could easily have justified myself in going "over the wall." It seemed to me that people like Jones needed to be institutionalized, not me. Thank God that place was escape-proof, because I was absolutely certain that if it wasn't, I might have made a break from that "Alcatraz."

I had fasted for days on end and prayed like there was no tomorrow. Since my arrival at the H.O.C. two months earlier, I had helped bring many hopeless men to Christ. The men's weekly prayer meeting had brought many of them into a more sincere walk with Jesus. The Bible studies saw a significant increase in attendance and participation, and many spiritual leaders stood toe-to-toe with me, including head Chaplain Sorenson who even gave me his personal recommendation. My new friends, Mark and Pam Jefferson and Hank, were constant reminders to me of God's unfailing love.

God had moved bountifully by giving me such a kind, tenderhearted lawyer as Sandy, who stood firm and undaunted, like an iron pillar, on behalf of Kristi and me. He gave me Wilke and Pearson as faithful friends and supporters. They were men of their word and often visited me in jail. He brought Pastor Rodgers into my life. His godly counsel and encouragement helped sustain me when things got rough. There were other soldiers who also joined hands and helped this warrior "Fight the good fight of faith." But now, after sixty-nine days, my anger and frustration about my circumstances was almost inconsolable.

The Major reason I was so distraught and uptight was that my wife was exactly nine-months pregnant, so our baby was due at any time. I had hoped for a breakthrough in court, but my situation looked even more hopeless now than it ever had. We received another two-week postponement, but we still had not even come close to a trial, or anything that even remotely resembled one. I had never witnessed such a deplorable waste of time, money, and energy as I had seen in my case.

In regard to Larry Jones, what can be said? His stand against me was vicious and totally unwarranted. I had never crossed the path of such a wrathful man in all my life. I hoped and prayed that he didn't treat his other clients with as much deplorable contempt as he had treated me. I would hate to be in his shoes and have to look at myself in the mirror every day trying to find a reason, any reason at all, to continue to live. I prayed that God would have mercy on him, even though he had shown none to me.

I called Kristi that night and encouraged her that God was still on His throne and that He would not fail us. We couldn't forget how He had spoken to me in prayer totally assuring us, beyond any doubt, that I would be set free before the birth of our baby. God had also confirmed this promise through Bea Ellen's glorious vision of us and the baby. There were many other people that were holding us up in prayer as well.

15

It's All Because
Of Jesus

In less than a week, I would be going to court again. All of our hopes and prayers were hanging on that day because Kristi would then be nine and one-half months pregnant. On that day, April 16, 1985, I would have spent eighty-two consecutive days in jail, and if God was going to move at all, He had to move on that last and final day. Unless God intervened now, my case would be postponed again. No doubt the baby would be born without my being there, and our prayers would be dashed. I knew how earnestly Kristi had prayed and sought the Lord. If I wasn't released in time, she would be severely hurt.

Pastor Rodgers had previously told me he would come to visit. At first, I thought it would be great to see him, but I was so guilt-ridden, having allowed bitterness, anger, and resentment to come into my heart, that I decided I didn't want to see him at all. I hated the justice system and those who represented it. Because of Larry Jones and his relentless probation hold, it appeared that my upcoming court date would be like all the rest with absolutely nothing being accomplished – no trial, no bail considerations, no hold release, nothing – just one postponement after another. In addition, the baby could come at any minute. At that moment, I felt very bitter toward Jones and a system that had no capacity to forgive. I had done nothing to deserve Jones's cold-blooded cruelty, and he was the primary reason I was still serving time.

It was Good Friday, and a visitor had come to see me. I

walked, angry and disheartened, to the visitor's room to find Pastor Rodgers waiting there for me. The moment he saw me he said, "Tom, you look so sad. What's wrong?"

"Pastor Rodgers, I'm sorry," I said, frustrated. "I've allowed bitterness and hate to enter my heart because I haven't been released. That Jones and his probation hold! I wish I could get him in a boxing ring for just one minute. I'd take his head off for all the grief he has caused me. I hate that man and this place! I'm no longer a criminal! I've given my life to Jesus, and it seems as though nobody cares! No one cares about me, my wife, or my baby. I'm very bitter, Pastor Rodgers! Won't you please pray for me?"

Pastor Rodgers answered, "Yes, Tom, I will, but first let me talk with you for a moment. I'm sorry that you've allowed hate and bitterness into your heart. It doesn't belong there, Tom. It belongs somewhere else."

"Where is that, Pastor Rodgers?" I asked.

"Tom it belongs on the Cross of Calvary. That is why Jesus came into the world. All of the bitterness, anger, and hate that we feel; all the pain, betrayal, and sorrow that you and I and others have to endure, all the suffering, sickness, and death that is in the world because of sin, it all belongs on the Cross. Jesus took it all, not just part of it, Tom. He took it all upon Himself. He is our sin-bearer. He is our substitute.

"We deserved to be punished and killed, not Him. All of us should have died and gone to hell because of our sin and rebellion against God. The Bible tells us in Romans 3:23, *'For all have sinned, and come short of the glory of God.'* And Romans 3:10 says, *'There is none righteous, no not one.'* In God's eyes, all of our own righteousness is like *'filthy rags'* and *'the wages of sin is death, but the gift of God is eternal life through Jesus Christ our Lord.'"*

"Tom, Jesus came into this world, a world that was created by Him and for Him; yet the world hated Him. He came to His very own people, Israel, the people He loved. They should have received their Messiah, but instead, they despised and rejected

Him, the very Author and Sustainer of life."

"Tom, Jesus endured so much more suffering than you or I could ever imagine, and He understands your anger and resentment. But because you belong to Him and because He has forgiven you of all your sins by washing them in His precious, cleansing Blood, you must also forgive Larry Jones. Tom, Jesus suffered on the Cross for you so that you would no longer have to carry the burden of your sin, anger, and hate. He bore our sins and sicknesses for us on Mt. Calvary that day. That is why, if we are true Christians, we can love when others hate, give when others take, and forgive when others condemn. It's because of Jesus, Tom. It's all because of Jesus."

"Pastor Rodgers," I said, "thank you for reminding me of what Jesus did for me. The Lord has touched my heart and given me great peace and assurance through your words. Now I can say that this is one of the best days of my life! Lord, I forgive those who have hurt me, and I especially forgive Larry Jones."

As Pastor Rodgers left, I promised Jesus that no matter what happened – even if I spent the entire twelve years in prison – I would be loving and forgiving all the days of my life. The revelation that I received from the Lord that day was a new and glorious beginning for me. For the first time, I was able to experience the awesome peace and glorious freedom available to me by allowing Jesus to help me forgive others, even those who are my worst enemies.

16

The Saddest
Day Of My Life

This was the big day! I was certain that the court appearance scheduled for today would be my very last one. I had called Kristi the night before and told her about my prior meeting with Pastor Rodgers and that I believed wholeheartedly that God was going to move mightily for us in court today. She felt very encouraged and was anxious for me to call her back to tell her when I would be flying back home after my release from jail. I went to court that day glowing with assurance. Even Sandy was surprised at my joyful countenance and said, "What's gotten into you?"

"Sandy, Jesus has gotten into me," I said with excitement, "It's all because of Jesus! I just know in my heart that God is going to work a miracle today. You just watch and see."

She looked at me doubtfully, "Well, Tom, expect your miracle, but we've got some serious problems right now with Larry Jones. Unless they're resolved, you're going nowhere. I hope you're right, but I just don't understand this faith thing that you have. I would hate to see you and Kristi crushed."

"You just watch what God does today, Sandy!" I said, beaming with confidence.

"Okay, Tom, I'm with you. You can be assured of that."

We walked into court that morning expecting a miracle. I couldn't wait to see Mr. Jones. The tenderness and forgiveness of God was burning in my heart, and I was ready to face him. I wanted to let him know how God had touched me on Good Friday and that no matter what he decided to do, I was still going to remain his friend and pray for him because I had truly forgiven him. *"And be ye kind one to another, tenderhearted, forgiving one another, even as God for Christ's sake hath forgiven you."* (Ephesians 4:32). I looked over at the D.A.'s table where he would be sitting, but he wasn't there. My case was called, and Mr. Jones was absent.

"Tom," Sandy said to me anxiously, "where's Jones? He has got to show up, or your case will be postponed again. You better start praying he walks in the door soon, or we're in hot water."

As my case file was being reviewed by the judge, the D.A. stood up and said, "Your honor, because Mr. Jones, the probation officer in this case, is not in the courtroom at present, I would move for an adjournment."

Sandy quickly responded, "Your honor, this matter has come before you a number of times now, and I had hoped that we could continue without Mr. Jones being here. My client has spent eighty-two days in jail waiting for the establishment of a bail bond that has been held up, primarily because of Mr. Jones, and for him to not be here for this case is completely unwarranted. Therefore, I would ask the court to grant bail for Mr. Wells because of Mr. Jones's failure to appear."

The judge replied, "Miss Ruffalo, you know the rules of the state and of this court. My hands are tied. I cannot release your client without his probation officer's approval. That's that. Case adjourned until May 1, at which time we will consider bail for your client. Is that understood?"

Sandy had no choice but to say, "Yes, Your Honor."

It was very difficult for me to accept, or even believe, what had just taken place. I wanted to scream out in total frustration, but it would have done no good. Sandy tried her very best to console me, but there was nothing that she or anyone else could say that would have relieved my anguish. All our hopes and prayers were now shattered completely, and I was numb.

Sandy spoke up, "Tom, listen to me for a minute. I know you're devastated right now, and I understand your pain. Tom, I've never told you this: I lost a son just a few years ago, and that pain was unlike anything I had ever known. I was swallowed up in unbearable sorrow for a long, long time. But Tom, God brought me through it, and God will bring you through this too. You and Kristi have been a source of strength for me, even though you may not have known it. I see your strong faith in God, and it overwhelms my heart. Tom, God is on your side, and He is not going to let you down.

"I know you have just received a major setback, but remember that you, Kristi, little Tommy, and your unborn baby are still alive. Rejoice that you will live to see another day. The days that are ahead for you will shine forth like the "Morning Star," and there is nothing that can stand in the way of the God that you serve. He will remove all obstacles and hindrances out of the way for the person that truly loves Him. Tom, I know that you love God. There's no question in my mind about that. You just watch and see what God is going to do for you and your family. Tom, I love you and Kristi, and we have another shot at this thing in two weeks, so don't give up."

Sandy's words of tenderness and encouragement were just what I needed to hear. After she spoke to me, I was put on the jail bus and brought back to the H.O.C.

I still had a grievous problem on my hands. I dreaded having to tell Kristi that our prayer for my release wasn't answered. I knew that I would have to call her and break the heart-wrenching news. I just didn't have the answers as to why God didn't intervene in our behalf. This would be the most difficult phone call of my entire life. The disappointment would absolutely crush her faith. I was afraid that it could even bring on her labor.

I knew that she was waiting by the phone, and I couldn't delay any longer. *God, please help me speak the right words to Kristi so that she will not be completely crushed,* I prayed. *Help me, Lord, to console her in this dark hour.* I dialed our number and waited for her answer.

I heard Kristi's voice say, "Hello?"

"Hi, darling, it's me! Kristi, listen, I'm calling from jail. I don't know how to tell you this, but I've got some bad news. Court didn't go as planned, but I'm confident God is still going to work a miracle for us. I don't know why He hasn't released me yet. It could be because He's moving so powerfully among the inmates here at the H.O.C. and that He wants me to continue to win more souls for Him here, or perhaps He has another plan. I just don't know. But I do know I love you and Tommy. Our new baby will be coming into the world shortly, and I will be home as soon as God releases me."

Kristi's voice was breaking when she sobbed, "Tom, why didn't God hear us? Why didn't He answer? We have prayed and fasted and sought the face of the Lord faithfully all this time, and now this happens! I just can't go on. Who will be with me in the hospital for the birth of our baby? No one! I'm all by myself! You said you had bad news. Well, I've got some too. I just left the doctor's office, and he said there is a good chance the baby will be born tonight. If not, he said that because I am two weeks overdue, they would induce labor so that the baby will be born tomorrow. Tom, this is terrible! This is the worst news that I have ever received. I'm just all confused right now. Considering all of the confirmed promises from the Lord, and everything else, I just don't know what to believe anymore!"

I urged her, "Kristi, don't give up – don't throw in the towel just yet! I know that God is on our side. Somehow, He will come through for us. God's Word has told us that it is impossible for Him to lie. Numbers 23:19 says, *'God is not a man, that He should lie, neither the son of man, that He should repent, hath He said, and shall He not do it? or hath he spoken, and shall he not make it good?'* God told us that He was going to get me out, and He is going to do it. I can't say when, but it will be soon, and then we will be back together. Kristi, all I ask is that you wait for me until God gets me out of here. Will you wait for me?"

"Yes, Tom, I will wait for you until the day God brings you back to me," she said, trying to hold back tears.

"I'll call tomorrow. You and the baby will constantly be in my prayers. Good-bye, my love."

I will never forget that phone call as long as I live. This was the saddest day of my life.

17

Not By Might,
Nor By Power,
But By My Spirit

I went to bed that night anguishing in prayer for Kristi, praying that if she had the baby, all would go well until I got there. I went to sleep that night in deep sorrow, just as Jesus' disciples had done the day He was crucified and before they had experienced the joy of His resurrection.

I was rudely awakened from a sound sleep at about 4:30 am the following day. I heard the words, "Get up, Wells," as the dorm sergeant briskly shook my arm. "You're going to court this morning."

I was half asleep and said groggily, "It's a mistake. I'm not scheduled for court today."

He said, "I've got you on the court calendar for this morning, so you've got to get up."

"No, sir. You're making a mistake here. I can show you. I was in court yesterday, and the judge postponed my next court date until May 1. That's two weeks from now. Here is my court date slip from the judge."

"I don't care about you slip," he said. "All I care about is you getting on that bus. Do you hear what I'm saying?"

Still half asleep, I was becoming irritated. "Would you listen for a minute! I'm not scheduled for court today, and I don't want to go! This has happened to me twice before, and I promised myself it wouldn't happen again. I don't want to go and sit in that filthy bullpen all day long simply because your computer system or your secretaries have made a mistake! Now, I'm going back to sleep, and you can just go about your business."

The guard was getting impatient with me and said, "Don't tell me about my business, Wells! This is my business. If I don't have you on that bus this morning, I'll lose my job. Do you understand? Now either get on that bus, or I will have you shackled and *put* on that bus. And I promise you, you'll be in lock-down tonight if I have any more trouble out of you. Now get on that bus!"

"I don't care about your threats, your shackles, or you lock-down!" I was feeling very belligerent by now. "This is a mistake, and I don't want to go! I'm mad and I'm bad! My wife probably had our baby last night, and because of this corrupt system you guys run, I'm still in this place! Now, I'll get on that bus, but you and I will have it out when I come back tonight. Do you understand me?"

By this time, half the dorm was wide awake, and some of the men shouted out, "Tell him what it's all about, Montana! We're all sick and tired of going to that filthy bullpen all day long and not being called for court!" the men in my jail dorm had nicknamed me "Montana," and I had a number of them on my side because of their conversion to Jesus.

I knew that I was wrong to rebel against authority, and I repented to the Lord on the hour-long bus ride to court.

We arrived at the county jail about 7:30 am. I was put in a small holding cell by myself until I would be called for court. I was sure I wouldn't be called because I wasn't scheduled, but I hoped they would leave me in this cell until I could take a bus ride back to the H.O.C. later that day. This cell was clean and quiet, something that was unheard of in the Milwaukee County jail system. Man, I hated to hear all that inmate jive-time talk and the inflated stories that were spewed out by these so-called "players" who never played big time a day in their lives. They talked like they ran the world.

Well, I was upset. I figured the baby was born the night before, and because I was not able to be there, I felt the Lord had let me down. I knew He was on my side, but at that moment I had no control over my frustration. It was now 8:30 am, and soon they would be calling the first bus-load of men to court at 9:00 am. While I was sitting in my cell, the small window in the door slid open, and a voice that sounded like my attorney called out, "Tom, are you here?"

I got up, surprised, and looked to see Sandy's face peering through the hole in the door.

"Yes, Sandy, I'm here. What are you doing here?"

"Tom," she said, "that's exactly the question I wanted to ask you. We were here yesterday, right?"

"Yeah, Sandy, that's right."

"We did receive a two-week postponement, didn't we?" She continued, "I don't understand this at all. All I know is that I was called early this morning and told to be in court for you, but I wasn't given any explanation why. This has got to be another mistake. Listen, I'm going to find out what's going on. I'll be back within fifteen minutes, and if I can, I will try to get you on the first bus out. All right, Tom?"

After Sandy left, I prayed she could get me on the first bus out. I didn't want to hang around there all day long if I could avoid it.

About ten to twelve minutes had gone by, and Sandy appeared in the window again. With tears welling up in her eyes, she said, "Tom, I don't know how to tell you this – I really don't know what to say – but in all my law career, I have never witnessed anything like this. Tom, your friends, those vice cops, Wilke and Pearson, are out in the courtroom petitioning before the judge for mercy and leniency toward you. They're asking the judge to please release you from jail so that you can be with your wife. They have told the judge that they would put their jobs on the line for you because they know, beyond question, that you are no longer a criminal or a danger to society and that your life has been changed because of Jesus Christ. Tom, in just a few minutes, you will be called before the judge, and you can see for yourself what these officers are trying to do."

As Sandy began to tell me about how Wilke and Pearson were unexpectedly there to help me, I instantly felt the awesome power and presence of God come upon me. The anointing of God shot straight through me like a powerful jolt of electricity. I could feel His glorious presence all over me, and the Holy Spirit clearly said, ***"Your miracle has come. I told you I would not let you down. Today you will be released from jail and go home to be with your wife for the birth of your child."***

I walked into the courtroom, and there they were, Mr. Wilke and Mr. Pearson. When my eyes met theirs, I saw the heart and courage of these valiant men, fighting for me as though I were their own son. They were pleading before the judge and the D.A. for my probation hold to be overturned. My case was then called, and I stood before Judge Stein, one of the most fair, yet severe, judges in the Milwaukee County court system.

He said, "Mr. Thomas Wells, in all my years as a judge, I have never seen a case like yours before. You're on probation hold because you left the state of Wisconsin and didn't notify Mr. Larry Jones, your probation officer. It also appears that you fled the state because of two pending charges of delivery of narcotics to an undercover police officer. You are on hold now because of your probation violation, and also, you haven't been given bail for these current cocaine charges. Is that correct?"

"Yes, Your Honor, that's correct," I responded. "In regard to fleeing the state, I honestly had no knowledge of any drug charges that were filed against me. I moved to Montana to start my life over again. And that's the truth, Your Honor."

"Well, I have no way of knowing if that's the truth or not, Mr. Wells," he continued, "but this is the part that I just don't believe. In the courtroom today, there are two high-ranking detectives with the vice squad department. These men have extradited you from Montana to face your cocaine charges here in Milwaukee, and they stand here pleading with me to have lenience toward you so that you can go home to be with your wife for the birth of your child. They have even gone so far as to put their jobs on the line for you, telling me that your life has been changed for the better and that you are no longer a criminal, but a Christian. I can certainly sympathize with your current dilemma, Mr. Wells. If my wife were pregnant, I would also want to be with her, but we have a problem here that I cannot overcome.

"This courtroom takes into consideration all testimony that's been given. However, when I hear what these two officers have to say about you, and when I receive testimony from experienced vice squad members who put their lives on the line on a day-to-day basis and have many years on the force, I take that kind of testimony into very serious consideration. To have it come from arresting officers who are trying to put the same man into prison is mind-boggling, to say the least. I would really like to help, but there is a problem. You are on a probation hold with Mr. Jones, and I have no power or authority over a probation hold.

"Now, I am going to call Mr. Jones to testify. If he changes his mind on the hold, that's another story; then I could help.

"Mr. Jones, would you come to the front, please."

For a few moments, there was complete silence in the courtroom as we waited for Jones to go up front. Finally, the D.A. stood up and said, "Your Honor, Mr. Jones, is not here today, and I have no way of knowing when he might arrive. I know that he received a call to appear today, but I can't tell you why he's not here."

The judge then asked, "What is the status with Mr. Wells in regard to Mr. Jones?"

The D.A. answered, "Mr. Jones has had Mr. Wells on hold for eighty-three days, and it is my belief that he has no intention, whatsoever, of releasing him. He intends to hold him for a full year for fear he might flee again to avoid prosecution on the cocaine charges."

"I see," the judge said. "Well, that's it, then. There's nothing that I can do. He's on irrevocable hold. Until Mr. Jones releases him, my hands, as a judge, are completely tied. I'm sorry, Mr. Wells, but there is absolutely nothing that can be done."

It appeared that all hope was gone, but I knew God had told me He was going to perform a miracle. I also knew what God said in Zechariah 4:6, 'Not by might, nor by power, but by My Spirit, saith the Lord of Hosts."

Then the D.A. stood up and said, "Your Honor, if I may, I would like to address the court. There is something that can be done for Mr. Wells. This is what I can propose, if the court would allow me."

The judge said, "You may proceed."

"Thank you, Your Honor. There is a state law that specifies if a probation officer is called to court and does not appear, the D.A. can take over the case. Accordingly, I would like to take over Mr. Wells's case, with your permission, Your Honor. I have also heard the testimony of Mr. Wilke and Mr. Pearson, and I find it totally overwhelming. Mr. Jones has ruled against Mr. Wells, but I want to overturn that decision and show mercy in this case so that he can be with his wife for the birth of their child."

The astonished judge exclaimed, "Now, this *is* unbelievable! First, I have the arresting officers come to court and testify in behalf of Mr. Wells, and now the D.A. has also joined their side. I guess the only one that you need now is me. Well, I'm coming over to his side too. Let's see what we can do to get this case off his record.

"Mr. Wells, in your file it says that you caused criminal damage to property by taking a brick and vandalizing a Mr. Hansen's car, causing damage in excess of twelve hundred dollars. You were quite a character in your past life, weren't you? This is what I'm going to do. I know that you can't come up with that kind of money to pay off this insurance debt, so I'm going to lower the amount you must pay to seven hundred fifty – no, five hundred – or, rather, make it three hundred dollars. Mr. Wells, can you come up with three hundred dollars in cash?"

"No, Your Honor, I can't," I said.

"Suddenly, in the far back row of the courtroom, an old woman stood up and said, "Judge, that man before you is my grandson, and I raised him most of his life. If you would take a check from me, I will pay the three-hundred-dollar cost for that car. And I can assure you, the check is good.""

"Excuse me, ma'am, did you say this boy is your grandson?"

Grandma Ott answered, "Yes, Judge, Tommy is my grandson."

"Well, this *is grand!*" the judge exclaimed. "Young man, it appears that everyone, including your grandma, is on your side today. Today appears to be your lucky day. If Grandma can go to bat for her grandson, then so can I. Grandma, if you will come up front to the bailiff and make out that check, I will close this case and release Mr. Wells to the authorities."

"Now, Mr. Wells, I've released you, but you still must appear before Judge Graham on the cocaine charges. Normally, bail will not be granted for narcotics charges, but after what I've seen here in this courtroom today, it appears that there is nothing that could hold you in jail."

There was a victory shout in the courtroom that sent chills down my spine and was heard all through the building. People were dancing, weeping, and embracing one another. The love of Christ was evident everywhere you looked. The D.A. was hugging the judge; Wilke and Pearson were hugging Sandy; and I was hugging everybody. Somehow, all these friends and relatives had been called to this last-minute court hearing. Even complete strangers that were waiting for other cases to be called were swept away in the excitement and were hugging one another.

I saw God do a miracle in the hearts of all of these wonderful people, right before my eyes. It was truly a miracle that Jones didn't show up! There is no doubt that he would have ruled against me, but God stopped him from being there. If Jones wouldn't let God soften his heart to change his mind and release my probation hold, then He just moved him out of the way and did not allow him to appear. Instead, God softened the hearts of the D.A. and a strict Jewish judge to rule in my favor. They had compassion on me and ruled in my favor, even though I deserved to be punished. This was all too overwhelming for me, and I knew that Judge Graham didn't stand a chance against the power of God's Holy Spirit that day.

Sandy stood there silently in awe at what had taken place in a matter of just fifteen minutes. For eighty-three days, I had been in jail and she had witnessed, firsthand, nothing happening. Now, in only a few minutes, God accomplished the impossible by shaking the Milwaukee County court system like it had never been shaken before.

Sandy finally regained her composure and said, "Tom, this tops it all! I'm speechless! Nothing I've ever seen even comes close to this! But remember, we have got to keep our cool. We still have another case ahead of us, and that will be called in fifteen minutes. The sheriff deputies are going to take you now, and I will see you in Judge Graham's courtroom. Tom, this is another tough case that we have ahead, but after what I've seen, nothing is too difficult for God."

Many of the spectators left that courtroom to follow us to Judge Jean Graham's courtroom and see the final outcome of my case. This was the greatest courtroom setting anyone could imagine. I was thinking, *Perry Mason, watch out! Matlock, watch out! Judge Jesus has just entered the room, and His train has filled the temple!* It says in Genesis 8:25 that Abraham said, *"Shall not the Judge of all the earth do right?"* God, the Righteous Judge, was going to do right by me, His servant, and no courtroom or human judge could stand in His way.

I was led into the courtroom where I was seated next to Sandy, and there I saw Wilke and Pearson, my friends, pleading for compassion and leniency before Judge Graham and a different representative from the D.A.'s office who was handling my other case.

My case was called, and Judge Graham began to comment, "Mr. Wells, I have already heard what took place in Judge Stein's courtroom. No doubt you're expecting me to follow suit here today, but I don't move that way. I'm going to hear all of the facts myself before I even consider bail. As far as I'm concerned, you fled the state, and until I can see things in a different light, I won't grant bail."

It looked bad for a moment, but I knew that once Wilke and Pearson spoke, her heart would also be softened. One by one, my vice squad friends each began to speak his heart to the judge.

Pearson said, "Your Honor, we make every effort to put men like Thomas Wells behind bars for as long as we can, but I can assure you that if Mr. Wells is released on bail so that he can go home for the birth of his child, he will appear in court when you tell him to be here. I stand on what I'm saying because I know that his life has been changed by God. He's no longer a criminal, and I not only vouch for his credibility, but I will put my job on the line that he will come back for trial on these cocaine charges."

Then Wilke stood up and said, "Your Honor, Mr. Pearson and I have both been on the force for over twenty years and are highly decorated vice squad officers. During our careers we have put many drug dealers in prison/ that's our job, and we love what we do. Mr. Wells was no different. We both had a very strong personal interest in his arrest and conviction.

"When he was arrested in Montana, we couldn't wait to go and get him. There was no question about it. We wanted him! We dropped everything to bring him back ourselves because we didn't want anything to go wrong. That's how badly we wanted him."

"On the plane ride back, he told us everything about his life and how God had miraculously intervened on his behalf to save him. We came to Montana as his enemies, but after hearing his soul-stirring testimony, we became his friends. I know it sounds and looks crazy for the arresting officers to testify on behalf of the man they are going to court against, but I can attest to this man's sincerity and change of heart. You can check my record if you wish. I have never gone to bat for a drug pusher until today."

"Your Honor, I am personally asking you to please give him a chance to be with his wife for the birth of their baby. I can assure you that he will come back for sentencing on these drug charges. I am willing to put my job and reputation on the line as a character witness for Mr. Wells in this matter."

I was deeply moved as Pearson and Wilke spoke about me being their friend. When they were finished speaking on my behalf, Judge Graham said, "Miss Ruffalo and Mr. Wells, would you please stand.

"In all of my years as a judge, I have never witnessed anything like this. According to the law, I should throw the book at you, Mr. Wells, but something in my heart is speaking differently. It's speaking mercy and compassion.

"After much consideration of this case, I've found the testimony of Mr. Wilke and Mr. Pearson to be the prevailing factor in my judgment. To have these arresting officers here to testify is something that is most overpowering and compelling. To see that they are so concerned about you and your family is very moving and very touching. I'm a mother, and I can relate to what is happening here."

"I'm going to move in favor of Mr. Wells. I know this will get some criticism, but frankly, I don't care. I feel confident that the defendant will be in court on his assigned date. Mr. Wells, I am releasing you on your own recognizance, and you will be expected to appear in court in three months. Now, get home quickly to your wife so that you don't miss the birth of that baby. Case adjourned."

The courtroom erupted in shouts of victory and praise. Everyone, from the court reporter to the bailiff, from the judge to the D.A., from the cops to the attorneys, was hugging and embracing one another in godly love. Everyone present witnessed the Holy Spirit move in the hearts of everyone in the courtroom in an unprecedented way.

God had intervened on my behalf just as He promised He would. He told me to pray so that I would be released from jail in time for the birth of our baby, and now it had happened. Oh, how great and glorious and magnificent is thy Name, Oh, Mighty, Mighty God!

All parties involved in my release congratulated me with bear hugs and kisses. I was enveloped by the love and mercy of my God and Savior, Jesus Christ, who never once let me down. Pastor Rodgers hugged me and said, "Tom, I know you've got a lot to do and you do not have much time. You will need a vehicle, so here are the keys to the church's van. Would you please come to the church tonight and share your miraculous testimony of God's delivering power?"

"Thank you, Pastor Rodgers, for everything," I said. "Yes, I will be there."

My faithful mother and grandmother warmly held and kissed me and said, "Tom, this is the greatest day of our lives. Meet us at the house, and you can make all the reservations for your trip home from there."

I left the courthouse and jumped into the van. I headed straight to my grandmother's house, which had also been my home as a teenager. As I drove, I found it difficult to completely grasp all that had just taken place. It all happened so fast that I didn't have time to really get a handle on it. But I knew that I was a free man, and I was homeward bound.

First, I needed to call Kristi and tell her about the glorious miracles that God had performed in court that day. I knew I would have to be tactful in case she hadn't already had the baby. I didn't want the excitement of hearing my unbelievable testimony to trigger her labor. I also had to make the necessary plane reservations for the first available flight to Kalispell, Montana.

Twenty minutes later I arrived at my grandmother's home and ran into the house to call Kristi to tell her what happened. As I walked in, the phone rang, and my grandma answered, "Hello? Oh, Kristi, how are you? It's been a few months since we last talked. I know that you want to speak with me, but there's someone here that needs to speak with you more than I do."

My grandma handed me the phone, and I said, "Kristi, darling, it's me!"

"Who is this?" she asked, very puzzled.

"Kristi, it's me, your husband!"

"Where did I call? This can't be happening!" she said in amazement.

"You called Grandma's."

"But you're in jail!" she exclaimed.

"No, Kristi," I said. "God has worked a miracle for us, and He has answered our prayers. I was released just a half hour ago, and I am coming home."

"But how? It's impossible," she said excitedly. "You weren't scheduled for court for another two weeks!"

"I know. I will explain it all later. But first, tell me, did you have the baby yet?"

"No, not yet, but any time now," she answered.

"Hold on, because I'm coming home. You can't have that baby until I get there!"

"I'll hold on," she assured me. "You just get here as soon as you can."

"I'm going to call for plane reservations right now," I said, "so wait right there and don't go anywhere until I call you back to give you all the flight information."

"Where am I going, nine and one-half months pregnant, silly? Tom, this is the most wonderful news I've ever heard! God did it! He didn't fail us! I will never forget this as long as I live."

I called the airlines and found out that the only flight to Kalispell for that day had already left, but there was one flight scheduled to depart at 8:05 am the following day which would arrive in Kalispell at 11:15 am. I made the reservation for that flight and called Kristi with the schedule. Then I told her the wonderful story of God's great and mighty deliverance. She wept as she heard how the Lord had intervened and made it possible for me to return home.

After that call, I shared with our many faithful supporters what God had done, and they all were spellbound at the greatness of our God. That night I went to Pastor Rodgers' church, and after his sermon, he asked me to share my personal testimony of God's faithfulness to His children and the miracle he had just performed for me. The congregation was filled with the glory and awe of God as I shared how God had made a way for me when there was no way.

18

Only God Can
Deliver Like That

After saying good-bye to my loving mom, my steadfast grandmother, and my faithful family and friends who stood by us these trying days, I boarded the plane headed for home. For eighty-three days I had waited on God, expecting Him to super-naturally intercede for me. I knew that He had spoken His Word to my heart, but there still were times that I experienced anguishing fear, frustration, and unbelief; at other times, He filled me with exuberant faith, confidence, and bold assurance. Yet in the midst of the fear and doubt, God still performed His wonders for my family and me just as He had promised He would. Psalms 136:4 says, *"To Him who alone doeth great wonders for His mercy endureth forever."* Only He could have performed this mighty wonder, and I would never cease from praising Him, for His mercy *does* endure forever.

I was overwhelmed with emotion as I got off the plane. I saw Kristi and Tommy instantly, and I ran to embrace them with all the love a husband could have for his wife and with all the compassion a father could have for his son.

I then understood just how Peter felt when he was delivered from prison by an angel of the Lord and had difficulty believing it was true. At first, he thought it was a vision or a dream but then realized that God had actually sent His angel to set him free. This whole episode seemed like a dream. But once I held Kristi and Tommy in my arms, I knew it was real, and I thanked the Lord who also set me free from my captivity,

We went straight to our home, the small trailer that Kristi had gotten for us, and spent that entire day and evening relishing the time together. I ate my wife's home cooking for the first time in eighty-four days, and it sure topped the food at the H.O.C. We laughed and played together until about eight in the evening when Kristi remarked, "Tom, it's time to go."

"Go where?" I asked.

"To the hospital. It's time. We're going to have a baby tonight. I can feel it!"

I thought she was joking and said, "Come on, Kristi, You're kidding, right? I just got off the plane."

"Tom, I'm not joking? We're going to have our baby. Let's go!"

We went straight to the hospital in Whitefish where the doctor would be waiting for us. This was too much to believe, but it was happening right before my eyes. For the next two and one-half hours, while Kristi was in intense labor, I prayed with the same fervency as Hezekiah did when he turned his face toward the wall and prayed to the Lord. I knew the nurses thought I was crazy, but I didn't care. I was an eyewitness to a miracle from the Lord, and I felt like praying up a storm that night.

This labor was more difficult than when Tommy was born – and he was rough. Kristi needed all the prayer that I could give her. At 11:15 that night, our boy was born. He was a handsome, strong, healthy baby. We decided to name him Daniel because he and his mother and I had been in a lion's den for eighty-three consecutive days. Praise the Lord! God shut the lions' mouths so that they could do us no harm.

Seconds after Daniel's birth, the Holy Spirit clearly spoke to me, saying, *"Tom, I could have released you the first day, the second day, or the third day. I could have released you the first week, the second week, or the third week. I could have released you the first month or the second month. But Tom, I waited to the very end – until it was absolutely humanly impossible for you to be released for the birth of your son – so that you would know, beyond question, that I am the God who delivered you. I am a God of miracles, and I wanted you to know that I can do anything! What I did for Daniel in the lions' den, I have done for you. What I did for Shadrach, Meshack, and Abednego in the burning, fiery furnace, I have done for you. What I did for Moses and the Children of Israel at the Red Sea, I have done for you. You will go to many that have given up on hope. Yes, you will go to those with nothing to hold onto, those on the brink of death and destruction, and tell them that I am no respecter of persons.* (He does not favor one person over another). *If they will trust Me and believe in Me and put their faith and confidence in the God who cannot fail, then I will also do for them what I have done for you this night."*

"But Lord, I don't understand. I'm all confused right now. I have wavered in my faith and let You down. When I went to court on the eighty-second day and my case was postponed again, I was devastated and had totally given up all hope. I stopped believing for the miracle that you had promised us. God, I failed you, and yet You still performed this awesome miracle in answer to our prayer. Why, God? Why?"

"O My son, don't you know that for eighty-two days you trusted Me to do the impossible? You never gave up hope. Right up to the very end, you believed that I would release you from jail and bring you home to be with Kristi for the birth of Daniel. After the last adjournment, your faith was absolutely shattered, and I saw the pain that you and Kristi were experiencing because of your broken hearts. And I said, 'Enough is enough!' Even though your faith had faltered and failed, I Am the God who keeps His word and His promises. For eighty-two days you trusted Me with steadfast faith, and then for one day your faith failed. Am I the kind of God that would withhold this mighty miracle because of one day's unbelief? No, My son. I love you and your family with an endless and boundless love. I never would have deprived you of this great miracle because your heart fainted for a moment, saith the Lord of Hosts."

Epilogue

The Final
Sentencing

I told Kristi what God had spoken to me, and she also was in Holy Awe of the Greatness of our God. Both of us knew, beyond question that: *Only God Can Deliver Like That!*

Just a few days later, I testified at our church about God's miraculous deliverance and the words that he had spoken to me. Pastor Tom and the congregation were awed by my testimony. The Lord opened many doors for me to share this testimony, and many lives in Montana were dramatically changed and saved.

The weeks flew by quickly, and soon we prepared to leave Montana and head back to Milwaukee for the final sentencing on my drug charges. We loaded all of our belongings on a small trailer and drove cross-country with our two little boys in the back seat. We arrived safely, and I rented a two-bedroom apartment on the northwest side of the city. I immediately found a job as assistant store manager with a large grocery chain.

My first court appearance in Milwaukee took only a few minutes, and another date was set. All parties involved in my case were grateful and relieved that I had proven myself trustworthy by arriving on time for this initial hearing.

Because of Wilke and Pearson's friendship and testimony in court and the abundance of compassion Judge Graham exhibited in releasing me, both Sandy and I felt compelled to waive our rights to a jury trial and throw ourselves on the mercy of the court for final sentencing.

My final sentencing date had arrived, and nearly a year had passed since my initial release. Many friends and family members were present in court that day. I came with Kristi and our two little boys, with all of our hopes and prayers for the future on the line for this last hearing.

God had given both Kristi and me a *"...peace of God which passeth all understanding..."* (Philippians 4:7) for the final sentencing. This would be the last chapter of my rebellious past, the epilogue of all the vile deeds and sins I had committed as a prodigal running from the Lord. After this day, the law could never bring accusation of wrongdoing against me ever again. I could be sentenced to twelve years in prison for the two counts of delivery of cocaine to an undercover police officer, and with my past criminal record, I was looking at a minimum of five years behind bars.

My past was an unfortunate mark against me, but because of the Lord, I had much more on my side. I knew the Lord could work for me as He worked for Jonathan and his armor-bearer when Jonathan said, *"It may be that the Lord will work for us. For there is no restraint to the Lord to save by many or by few"* (1 Samuel 14:6 The favor of the Lord was echoing so profoundly in the courtroom during my hearing that it was deafening to any who would listen. I had received many favorable references from men of outstanding character, and the fact that I was working a good job was strong evidence of my desire to live an honest, godly life. Pastor Rodgers and members of the church congregation were there to back me. Sandy was there as my attorney, but she was much more than that. She had told me that she would represent me as if I were her own son – and that she did. She poured her life out to help not only me, but my entire family as well. She was God's appointed attorney for me and would continue to be our friend for years to come.

As for Wilke and Pearson, I wanted to save the best for last. When Kristi, the boys, and I walked into the courtroom that day, I saw both vice squad detectives in the same place where I had left them a year earlier. They were standing in front of the bench where the judge was sitting, and they were there for a reason. They came not only to show their support, but they came to ask for something that only one person could give that day. They came to ask for mercy and leniency toward me, a man who had made a mistake in his past, who was truly sorry for what he had done, and who was trying the best he could to begin over again, with God's help.

Wilke and Pearson didn't have to do what they did for me, and I saw something in these men that spoke volumes to my heart. After all, they were cops. It was their duty to put criminals and hardened men behind bars, not testify on their behalf. They took incorrigible individuals who are beyond help and discarded them into a prison environment which usually makes men and women worse than when they came in. it was their job to help put away lawbreakers who hurt, maim, and corrupt others.

They came to Montana on that plane flight, more than a year ago, intending to put me away because I deserved to be slam-dunked. However, through the sincere, humble words I shared with them about how Jesus saved me when there was no hope left, and about how He changed me, they saw a hope for me that they had not seen before. I could not change myself, because I had no power or ability to change. But God, by His amazing grace, reached down and saved this wretch from destruction. They had never heard a testimony like that before, and God quickened their hearts to believe the story of a man who had fallen away from his Lord many years before. God, in His unrelenting love, had said, "Enough, devil. You can't have him anymore. Tom belongs to Me." Jesus saved me and healed me and put me on the straight and narrow road to be a witness for Him so that others could be saved by the testimony of His love in my life.

The judge said, "Thomas David Wells, you are here for final sentencing on two counts of delivery of cocaine to an undercover police officer. What is your plea to these charges?"

"Guilty, Your Honor."

"I find the defendant guilty as charged."

"Mr. Wells, I have had much time to closely deliberate your case and find it to be the most unique case that I have ever had. If you remember, I was the one who released you for the birth of your baby. I take it that the little one sitting with your wife is he."

"Yes, Your Honor, that's Danny," I said proudly.

The judge continued, "The thing that is so overwhelming in your case is the vice squad detectives' testimony. These men traveled across the country to extradite you to face these charges. They planned to testify against you in court, but something occurred on that plane trip that changed their hearts. In addition, they put their careers and reputations on the line by becoming your friends. They also testified as character witnesses for you in another courtroom on a separate case in which they were not even involved. They were even able to persuade a D.A. and a judge to help you. Now they have done the same thing in this courtroom, not just once, but twice."

"I hope you never forget the kindness these men, and others, have shown you. They were convinced on that plane trip that your life had been dramatically changed, and in dealing with you over the course of the past year, they have been further persuaded by your new lifestyle that you are no longer a risk to society. According to state law, I could sentence you to prison for twelve years for the crimes you have committed, and most judges would do just that. Do you understand me, Mr. Wells?"

"Yes, I do, Your Honor."

"Today, after all that I have personally witnessed this past year and all that I have heard about you and your family and the circumstances surrounding your case, coupled with all the testimony that I have heard in court, all I feel in my heart is burning compassion toward you."

I watched intently as the judge firmly gripped the gavel in her hand. I knew with unmistakable certainty that my future would be dramatically affected in the next few seconds. At that precise moment, I felt the full tormenting weight of my sin against my Holy God and society. My life and the lives of my loved ones were hanging in the balance and were literally in the hands of Judge Graham.

But I had an assurance deep in my heart that transcended anything I had ever known before. I was fully persuaded that Judge Graham was not the only judge in the courtroom. You see, there was another judge that presided over the courtroom that day, and His name is Jesus, my Savior and my Lord. He is called the Lord, the Righteous Judge, and Psalms 50:6 says, *"The heavens shall declare His righteousness: for God is Judge Himself."*

It appeared to all in the courtroom that the gavel of justice and my life were in the hands of Judge Graham. But by faith I had a bold, courageous confidence that my life was safe in the gentle hands of the Man from Galilee, the One who silenced the raging storm and calmed the stormy sea by saying, *"Peace be still,"* the elements are subject to Me; the One who turned the water into wine, restored hearing to the deaf, and gave vision to the blind; the One who cleansed the defiled leper, raised up the withered lame, and performed other notable miracles of that kind; the One who parted the Red Sea, shut the lions' mouths, and delivered His servants out of the burning fiery furnace so that all the earth could see; the One who died a horrifying death on the Cross of Calvary for you and for me. Then in faithfulness and magnificence, He arose from the dead just like He said. He triumphed victoriously, conquering disease, death, hell, and the grave. No, I wasn't in the hands of a human judge. I was in the hands of the Master that day. Isaiah 49:16 says, *"Behold, I have graven you upon the palms of my hands."* It was the hands of Jesus that held me safely and securely.

As I awaited Judge Graham's final sentencing, I felt like David who said in Psalms 142:6-7, *"Attend unto my cry; for I am brought very low; deliver me from my persecutors; for they are stronger than I. Bring my soul out of prison, that I may praise thy name..."*

With my head bowed and my eyes closed, I waited for the judge to pronounce my sentence.

Judge Graham said, "This is my ruling: I sentence you to eighty-three days in the House of Correction with full credit for the time you have already served. I am also going to reduce this case from a felony to a misdemeanor so that this criminal offense will never be on your official record. I am going to release you, Mr. Wells, without any probation, whatsoever. You are a free man! May God bless your life!"

Those last words spoken by Judge Graham that stated, "You are a free man. May God bless your life," were words that I would never forget as long as I live. I rushed to where Kristi and my two boys were sitting and threw my loving arms around them, engulfing them in kisses, caresses, and tears. The praises and worship of the Lord resounded throughout the courtroom. I could praise and sing out with David and others who had experienced and witnessed, firsthand, the great, awesome deliverance of the Lord. *Oh, Lord, You have delivered my soul from prison, and now I can praise Your Name!*

As the sound of the judge's gavel echoed throughout the courtroom, I truly knew who had actually rendered that glorious and miraculous decision. It was Judge Jesus who held the gavel of justice in His hand and who had come to set this captive free. Isaiah 42:5-7 says, *"Thus saith God the Lord, He that created the heavens, and stretched them out; He that spread forth the earth, and that which cometh out of it; He that giveth breath unto the people upon it, and spirit to them that walk therein: I the Lord have called thee in righteousness, and will hold thine hand, and will keep thee, and give thee for a covenant of the people, for a light of the Gentiles; To open the blind eyes, to bring out the prisoners from the prison, and them that sit in darkness out of the prison house."* and John 8:36 says, *"If the Son, therefore, shall make you free, ye shall be free indeed."*

As I walked slowly out of the courtroom totally victorious, with my boys nestled in my arms, and Kristi close by my side, many close friends and family members gathered around and congratulated us on our great victory in court. Tears of gratitude were streaming down my face, and I couldn't, for a moment, accept any merit for this awesome miracle. I humbly looked up to my Great, Glorious God and Mighty, Holy Redeemer, Jesus Christ, and raised holy hands *"To Him who alone doeth great wonders: for His mercy endureth forever."* I knew, unequivocally, beyond any question or doubt, that it was God alone who did this great wonder.

In the Book of Daniel, Chapter 3:29, we read about the miraculous deliverance of Shadrach, Meshach, and Abednego out of the burning fiery furnace. What made the miracle described in this Scripture all the more wonderful is that the heathen Babylonian King Nebuchadnezzar and many of his leaders were eyewitnesses to that unbelievable miracle. King Nebuchadnezzar was totally astounded at what had taken place and made this glorious proclamation: *"Therefore I make decree, That every people, nation, and language, which speak any thing amiss against the God of Shadrach, Meshach, and Abednego, shall be cut in pieces, and their houses shall be made a dunghill: because there is **no other God that can deliver after this sort.**"* And for the remainder of my life, I will also proclaim that...

Only God Can
Deliver Like That

THE END

A Personal Message From The Author

Jesus said, *"Because of the increase of wickedness and lawlessness, the love of many will grow cold. But he who stands firm to the end will be saved"* (Matthew 24:12-13). The dramatic increase of sin, violence, and iniquity in the world today has left many people callous, hardened, and indifferent to the plight of others. The increasingly chaotic world we live in is rushing headlong toward self-destruction and judgment. There is an accelerated decline in moral standards, and the love for God and His Holy Word is waning and growing cold in the hearts of many people. It is difficult to find anyone or anything that you can truly put your faith, trust, and confidence in. It is both rare and refreshing to find someone who really cares enough to unselfishly reach out to help relieve the painful suffering of others.

In the writing of this book, I have diligently labored to reach out and give hope to you through the graphic story about the real-life experiences that God has so lovingly and graciously taken me through. Without His merciful protection, I would not have survived to write this book. I would be both foolish and vain if I attempted to take any credit for any of the awesome things that God has allowed me to experience in my life. It was for this purpose (the writing of this book and others to come) that He has supernaturally brought me through extreme trials and tribulations (even though I did not deserve His help) so that you and others can see, in a very dramatic way, the unfathomable depth of His love, patience, and mercy for you, me, and each and every person that He has created and placed on this earth. Without His long-suffering, kindness, and supernatural intervention on my behalf on numerous occasions, I most certainly would be either dead, maimed, imprisoned for life, or in an asylum for the mentally insane. Because of the destructive, ruinous pathway I had chosen to walk down and the dreadful, rebellious lifestyle that I was pursuing, I was doomed to a fate of natural and spiritual death and eternal separation from God. I became hopelessly enslaved to the vile lusts and addictions that controlled me and was left with no hope, whatsoever, because I was totally unable (by my own strength, power, or self-will) to set myself free from these ravaging bondages.

My only hope was in my faithful, merciful God who never, ever abandoned or betrayed me. He possesses the unlimited power to rescue you and me from any peril or problem that we may face. Through the saving, precious, Holy Blood of His Son, Jesus Christ, my Savior and my Lord, shed for me on the Cross of Calvary, the countless sins and iniquities in my life were forgiven; the bondages and destructive strongholds over my life were broken; the evil curses overshadowing my life were crushed; my crimes and offenses against others were pardoned; the sicknesses and diseases in my body were healed; the pain and sorrow in my life were removed; the disgrace and shame in my life was silenced; the shadow of death over my life was demolished; the weaknesses and frailties in my life were strengthened my failures and mistakes were forgotten; the shipwrecks and broken dreams in my life were repaired; the joy and happiness in my life was rejuvenated; the soundness of my mind was recovered; my purpose and calling in life was renewed; my family and loved ones were restored; and the dreams and hopes in my life were revived.

God says in Joel 2:25-26, *"And I will restore or replace for you the years that the locust has eaten, the hopping locust, the stripping locust and the crawling locust, My great army which I sent among you. And you shall eat in plenty and be satisfied, and praise the name of the Lord, your God, who has dealt wondrously with you. And my people shall never be put to shame"* (Amplified Bible). Jesus has restored all these things to me, as He promised in this Scripture; and more importantly, He has given me eternal life together with Him. I will give Him glory, honor, and praise for having done all these things for me. I will forever (for all eternity) confess the love, mercy, awesomeness, greatness, and magnificence of my God who has saved me from the very pit of hell and from eternal separation from Him. He has truly transformed me into a totally new person as He promised He would in His Eternal Word, the Bible. *"Therefore, if any man be in Christ, he is a new creature: old things are passed away; behold, all things are become new"* (2 Corinthians 5:7).

I have written this book to share with you how Jesus

miraculously saved me, changed my life, and put His tender love and concern in my heart for you and everyone who crosses my path and to minister to those of you who are weary, disillusioned, depressed, wounded, rejected, helpless, hopeless, imprisoned and in bondage that *Jesus is your answer!* He is the great I Am, the only One who can miraculously change your life and destiny both now and for all eternity. He has placed a burning, compassionate desire within me to tell everyone that what He has done for me, He also wants to do for you, if you will open your heart and allow Him to come in and be the Savior of your life. God says in 2 Corinthians 6:2, *"Behold, now is the accepted time; behold, now is the day of salvation."* I am asking you, from the very depth of my heart, to please give God a chance in your life. You have earnestly tried everything else. You have relentlessly pursued every aimless, empty, and ineffective avenue that the world offers, and your efforts have made you bitter, angry, frustrated, weary, powerless, hopeless, and totally disillusioned.

Today, right now, you can find the answers that you have so diligently sought after but have been unable to find. Jesus said, *"I am the way, the truth, and the life; no man cometh unto the Father, but by me"* (John 14:6). The pathway that you have so passionately and persistently tried to find, the truth that you have so intensely and zealously searched for, and the life that you have so fervently and sincerely sought after can be found in none other than the Lord Jesus Christ. God says, *"… Is there a God beside me? Yea, there is no God; I know not any"* (Isaiah 44:8). You can know Him today as your personal Savior, Lord, King, and dearest, most trusted friend. He is a friend that sticks closer than a brother, a friend that loves at all times, and a friend that will never leave you nor forsake you. He is knocking at the very door of your heart and asking you to let Him come in. Jesus said, *"Behold, I stand at the door, and knock: if any man hear my voice, and open the door, I will come in to him, and will sup with him, and he with Me"* (Revelation 3:20).

God never forces Himself upon anyone. He didn't create us as obedient robots forced to do His bidding. He created us in His own image and likeness so that He may be glorified through our lives. He gives us a free will and the opportunity to choose to either receive the free gift of salvation and eternal life or to reject Him by continuing to go our own sinful way down the path of destruction. I had grieved my loving Heavenly Father for many years when I rebelliously and defiantly walked away from Him to go my own selfish way. But He never gave up on me or stopped loving me, and He openly welcomed me back into His loving arms when I repented of my sins and returned home to Him as the wayward Prodigal Son.

I am now going to ask you some very personal questions, the most important questions that anyone could ever ask you – because they have eternal consequences. Are you saved? Are you born-again, and are your sins forgiven and washed away by the cleansing, shed Blood of God's own Son? Is your name written in the "Lamb's Book of Life?" If your life were taken from you today, would you know, beyond any doubt, that you would spend all eternity in the glorious presence of your loving God? Or would you be doomed to experience an endless eternity of anguish, horror, and unspeakable suffering reserved for those who are "lost" and must (on their own) pay the penalty for their sins after they die? God's Word warns us that hell is a very real place located in *"outer darkness"* where there is an eternity of *"weeping and wailing and gnashing of teeth,"* where there are tormenting fires that are never quenched, and where the worms that will be crawling on you will never die. It is a place where you will be fully alert and aware of all your unspeakable torments. For all eternity you will remember the opportunities that you had, but rejected, during your lifetime to receive Jesus as your Lord and Savior so that you might be spared the torments of hell. We are all sinners, and God's Word is very clear about the penalty that must be paid by each of us for our sins. *"For the wages of sin is death: but the gift of God is eternal life through Jesus Christ our Lord"* (Romans 6:23).

Our Heavenly Father loves each and every one of us. He does not want us to be punished by eternal separation from Him. But because He is Holy and Righteous, He hates sin and cannot allow us to even come into His presence blemished by our sinful condition. The stain of sin must first be removed from us and the required death penalty paid before we can come near to Him. Through man's willful disobedience in the Garden of Eden, he brought the curse of sin, sorrow, and suffering upon himself and also upon the perfect, pure, sinless world that God originally created. In that moment of rebellion to God's commands, Adam and Eve opened the door to allow all of the sin and evil to enter into the world that we see all around us today. Man's ability to commune and fellowship directly with God was severed. In our sinful condition, there is absolutely nothing that any of us can do to remove the terrible stain of sin that is so offensive to our Heavenly Father. God's Word tells us that he looked throughout the entire earth and could not find even one "righteous" man and that our own best efforts to be good and righteous are as *"filthy rags"* (Isaiah 63:6) in His eyes. God looked down upon the sinful, evil condition of man, and His entire creation, and was seriously grieved that we, His children, had permanently cut ourselves off from Him because of our willful disobedience and sin.

The great, glorious news of the Gospel is that God loves us so much that He has provided a "redemption plan" which He offers to each of us as a way to escape our hopeless, sinful circumstance. In John 3:16 He says, *"For God so loved the world, that He gave His only begotten son, that whosoever believeth in Him should not perish, but have everlasting life."* Since no man was ever worthy or able to pay the debt for man's sin, Jesus, the magnificent Creator of the universe, agreed to step out of the glory of heaven to humble Himself and become a man so that He could pay our sin debt for us. Jesus, in obedience to His Father, knew that only His perfect sacrifice as a sinless man would satisfy the righteously pronounced judgment and penalty for your sin. Out of unfathomable love, He substituted Himself for you and me on the Cross of Calvary and shed forth His precious, cleansing Blood so that the vile, permanent stain of your sins could be washed away. You can be made clean and stand in His presence in clean and white garments, forever. God said, *"Come now, and let us reason together, sayeth the Lord: though your sins be as scarlet, they shall be white as snow; though they be red like crimson, they shall be as wool"* (Isaiah 1:18).

Jesus was the sinless, innocent "Lamb of God" who willingly and humbly allowed Himself to be led to the slaughter. Isaiah 53:3-7 describes the cruel, cold-blooded, and inhumane treatment that

Jesus received, as our substitute, when He was punished for your sins and the sins of the world. *"He was despised and rejected and forsaken by men, a Man of sorrows and pains, and acquainted with grief and sickness; and as one from Whom men hide their faces he was despised, and we did not appreciate His worth or have any esteem for Him.*

"Surely He has borne our griefs – sickness, weakness and distress – and carried our sorrows and pain [of punishment]. Yet we ignorantly considered Him stricken, smitten and afflicted by God [as if with leprosy]".

"But He was wounded for our transgressions; He was bruised for our guilt and iniquities; the chastisement needful to obtain peace and well-being for us was upon Him, and with the stripes that wounded Him we are healed and made whole."

"All we like sheep have gone astray, we have turned every one to his own way; and the Lord has made to light (placed) on Him the guilt and iniquity of us all."

"He was oppressed, yet when He was afflicted He was submissive and opened not His mouth; as a lamb that is led to the slaughter, and as a sheep that before her shearers is dumb, so He opened not His mouth" (Amplified Bible).

No one has ever received the torture that our Savior endured that day – and He did it all for you and for me. He willingly did all of these things out of love so that you and I and every person on this earth might be forgiven in the eyes of our Heavenly Father and so that we might be able to spend all eternity with Him. God says, *"Without the shedding of blood, there is no remission of sin"* (Hebrews 9:22). His precious, cleansing blood was poured forth that day to provide the forgiveness and remission of our sins. There is a beautiful song whose title appropriately describes our Savior, entitled, "Any King Who Would Wear A Crown Of Thorns Is Worthy To Be Praised."

Through Jesus' sacrificial death and victorious resurrection, God offers you the "free gift" of salvation and eternal life if you believe in your heart and confess that you are a sinner separated from God; that Jesus is God's Son who was punished for you personally and died on the Cross of Calvary to pay for your sins and the sins of the world; and that he is your personal Lord and Savior. Salvation is an undeserved gift from God which cannot be earned or purchased at any price. God says, "For by grace are ye saved through faith; and that not of yourselves; it is the gift of God: Not of works, lest any man should boast" (Ephesians 2:8-9). The foundational truth of Christianity is that we are saved and justified in God's eyes through faith in Jesus' death and resurrection. You have God's promise which says, *"That if thou shalt confess with thy mouth the Lord Jesus, and shalt believe in thine heart that God hath raised Him from the dead, thou shalt be saved"* (Romans 10:9).

Jesus loves all of us so very much, no matter who we are or what we have done. He has promised us eternal life if we will repent and turn from our wicked sins and ask for His forgiveness. He will lovingly accept even the vilest sinner just as he is, wherever he is. No matter how far you have fallen away from God, and even if you have committed the most terrible sins imaginable, He is asking you to come to Him today to be forgiven and to be made pure and whole. If you sincerely come to Jesus and ask for forgiveness, He will never reject you or cast you aside. Jesus said, *"All that the Father giveth (entrusts) me shall come to me; and him that cometh to me I will in no wise cast out"* (John 6:37).

After you die, judgment is set, and it is too late to repent; so there is an urgency to His loving appeal to you today through this message. Jesus is knocking at the door of your heart today, and I earnestly implore you to let Him come in and change your life.

You can come to Jesus today to be forgiven and become a "new creature in Christ." You may not have another opportunity, so won't you please pray this prayer to Father God with me? This is a very personal matter between you and Him, and He knows your heart. If you are serious and sincere with Him in this prayer, you can know for sure, right now, today, that you are saved and have eternal life.

God said in 1 John 5:11-13, *"And this is the record, that God has given to us eternal life, and this life is in His Son. He that has the Son has life; and he that has not the Son of God has not life.*

These things have I written unto you that believe on the name of the Son of God; that you may know that you have eternal life, and that you may believe on the name of the Son of God." 1 John 2:25 says, *"And this is the promise that He has promised us, even eternal life."*

"Heavenly Father, I humbly come before You this day. I confess that I am in dire, desperate need of your mercy. I confess to You, gracious Father, that I am a sinner, and I have lost my way. But now I believe and have faith that through Your Son, Jesus Christ, I can find forgiveness for my sins and have eternal life. I ask you to forgive me for every sin that I ever committed and for my acts of rebellion and disobedience against you and my fellow man. Lord Jesus, I ask you to cleanse and wash away all of my sins with Your precious, saving Blood that You shed for me on the Cross of Calvary. I believe that You died for me, rose again from the dead, and are now seated at the right hand of my Heavenly Father as my mediator with Him. I ask you to come into my heart and to be the Lord of my life from this day forward. Now, by faith and trust in Your Holy Word, I believe that I am saved and that all of my sins have been forgiven. I thank You, Lord, for giving me the free gift of salvation, and I declare by the lips of my mouth and by the belief in my heart that Jesus Christ is my Savior, Lord, and King. In Jesus' Name I pray. Amen.

Love in Jesus' Name.

Miracles, Miracles, Miracles

Come and see
God's plan unfold,
Come and see Jesus Christ
Work miracles untold.

Come and see
What the Bible foretold,
As Jesus gives sight to the blind
As in the days of old.

Come and see
The cripples walk,
As the power of Jesus
Enables the "dumb" to talk.

Come and see
Arms and legs grow out,
When they are touched by Jesus
The maimed will dance and shout.

Come and see
Those who *were* palsied and lame,
Confess they were healed by Jesus
As when the first time He came.

Come and see
Those possessed by demonic powers,
As the spoken name of *"Jesus"*
Delivers them in that very same hour.

Come and see
The dead being raised,
As loved ones rejoice
Giving Jesus all the praise.

Come and see
Jesus awesome glory and power,
When it appears in the earth
At God's appointed hour.

Pardoned Forever

Sin is a prison
that many can't see,
and Satan is the jailer
who has captured me.

I committed no crime
to create my sin,
this is a prison
that I was born within

It's so dark in this prison
That the bars can't be seen,
tho I bathe in the sunlight
my soul is unclean.

The prison is spiritual
and my sentence is death,
unless I find Jesus
before my last breath.

He is the light
that allows me to see,
the bondage of sin
And my captivity

Jesus is the "Way"
the "Truth" and the "Light"
Only He can give
me spiritual sight.

Only He has the key
to unlock the door,
that will set me free
forevermore.

You, too, can be free
from your spiritual prison,
if you accept Jesus
As your Savior, arisen.

The poems <u>Miracles, Miracles, Miracles</u> & <u>Pardoned Forever</u>
Written by Fred C. Genrich *(With God's Help)*

"For the wages of sin is death; but the gift of God is eternal life
through Jesus Christ our Lord" (Romans 6:23).

"...If thou shalt confess with thy mouth the Lord Jesus, and thou
shalt believe in thine heart that God has raised him up from the
dead, thou shalt be saved" (Romans 10:9).

Credits:

Cover Photo adapted from the famous painting
Forgiven
By Thomas Blackshear

This edition of "Only God Can Deliver Like That"
compiled by Ed Lemberger – www.EdLemberger.com

Sketch on page ii by:
Amanda M. Cordoba

Only God Can
Deliver Like That

By Thomas David Redlich

In JESUS
Holy Name!

Made in the USA
Monee, IL
11 May 2021